PICKLES

A Cartoon Collection by Brian Crane

LONGSTREET

Atlanta, Georgia

Published by
LONGSTREET PRESS, INC.
A subsidiary of Cox Newspapers
A subsidiary of Cox Enterprises, Inc.
2140 Newmarket Parkway
Suite 122
Marietta, GA 30067

Printed in the United States of America

Library of Congress Catalog Card Number: 98-066374

ISBN: 1-56352-510-0

Cover illustration: Brian Crane
Cover and book design: Jill Dible

This book is dedicated to my mother, Helen, and my wife, Diana, without whose encouragement and support I would still be working for a living.

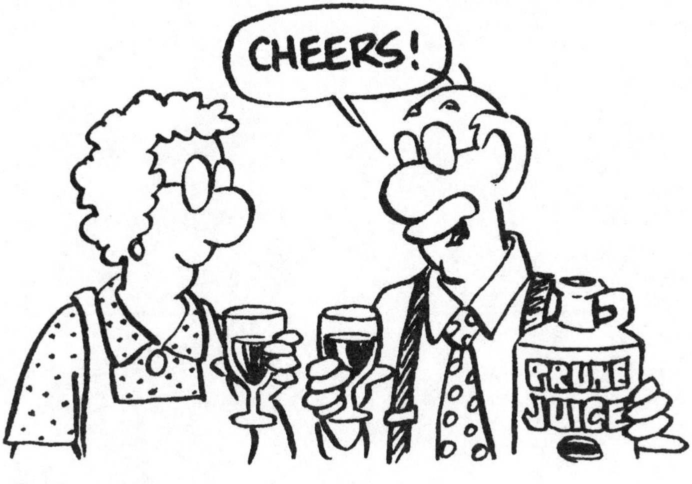
CHEERS!
PRUNE JUICE

FOREWORD

There are many things I like about Brian Crane's feature, *Pickles.* I think it would be very comforting to have Earl and Opal for neighbors. I can see myself going over to their house, having a cup of tea and maybe some sugar cookies, and talking about the old days, even though I have a feeling that they are not as old as I am. Maybe I could bore them with my own stories.

Pickles has a wonderful group of characters and, of course, I like the dog. I like the face that Brian draws on Roscoe. It's a good dog face, and it's fun to look at. Actually the whole strip is fun to look at, and I am convinced, as I have remarked about other features that I like, it is very important for the reader to want to look at a strip. Good drawing is good design and good design makes a feature attractive.

Pickles is going to be around for a long time, and I am glad we have this collection to look at over and over and over.

– CHARLES M. SCHULZ

PICKLES

PICKLES

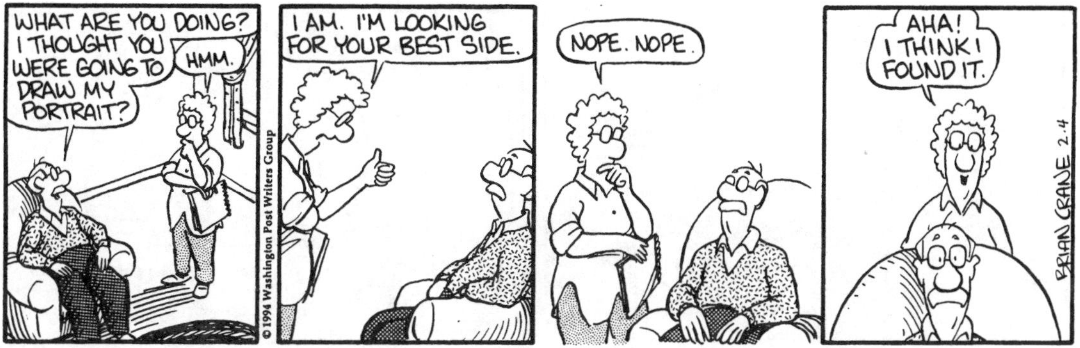
WHAT ARE YOU DOING? I THOUGHT YOU WERE GOING TO DRAW MY PORTRAIT?
HMM.
I AM. I'M LOOKING FOR YOUR BEST SIDE.
NOPE. NOPE.
AHA! I THINK I FOUND IT.
© 1994 Washington Post Writers Group
BRIAN CRANE 2.4

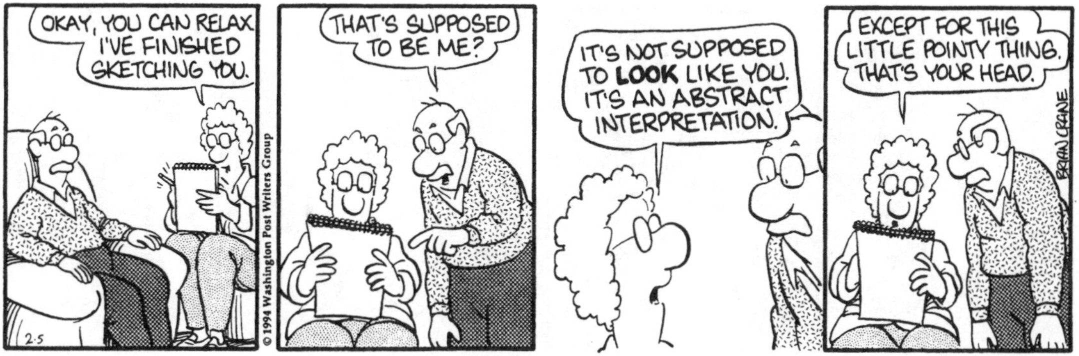
OKAY, YOU CAN RELAX. I'VE FINISHED SKETCHING YOU.
2.5
THAT'S SUPPOSED TO BE ME?
IT'S NOT SUPPOSED TO **LOOK** LIKE YOU. IT'S AN ABSTRACT INTERPRETATION.
EXCEPT FOR THIS LITTLE POINTY THING. THAT'S YOUR HEAD.
© 1994 Washington Post Writers Group
BRIAN CRANE

PICKLES

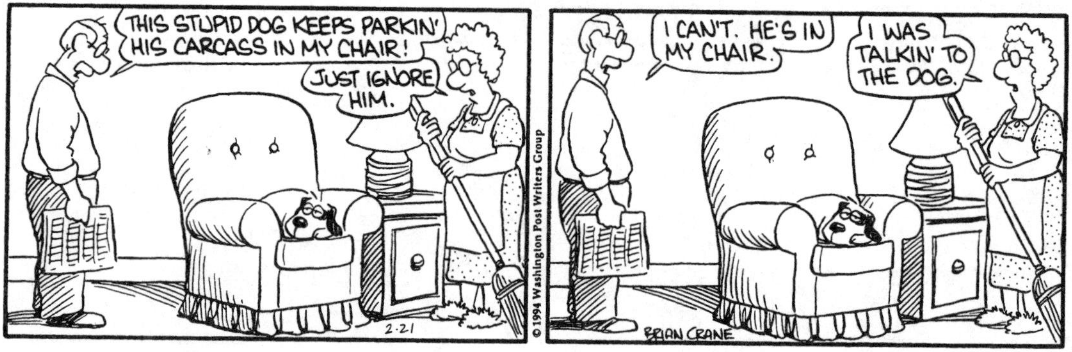

THIS STUPID DOG KEEPS PARKIN' HIS CARCASS IN MY CHAIR!
JUST IGNORE HIM.
2·21
© 1994 Washington Post Writers Group
I CAN'T. HE'S IN MY CHAIR.
I WAS TALKIN' TO THE DOG.
BRIAN CRANE

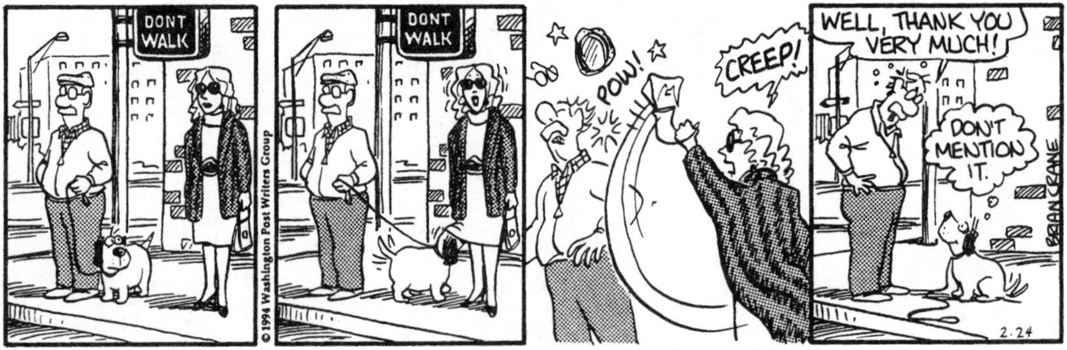

DONT WALK
© 1994 Washington Post Writers Group
DONT WALK
POW!
CREEP!
WELL, THANK YOU VERY MUCH!
DON'T MENTION IT.
BRIAN CRANE
2·24

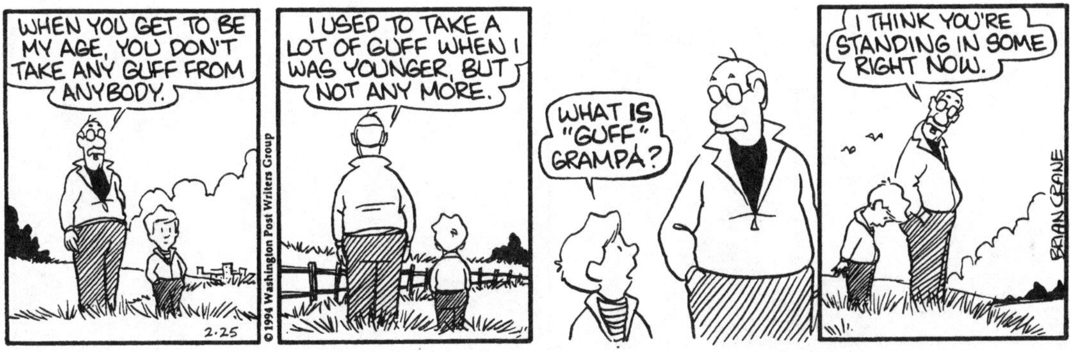
WHEN YOU GET TO BE MY AGE, YOU DON'T TAKE ANY GUFF FROM ANYBODY.
2·25
© 1994 Washington Post Writers Group
I USED TO TAKE A LOT OF GUFF WHEN I WAS YOUNGER, BUT NOT ANY MORE.
WHAT IS "GUFF" GRAMPA?
I THINK YOU'RE STANDING IN SOME RIGHT NOW.
BRIAN CRANE

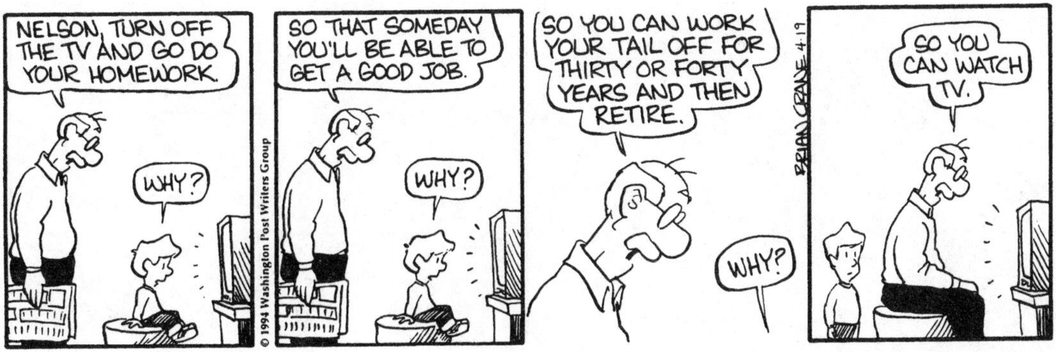
NELSON, TURN OFF THE TV AND GO DO YOUR HOMEWORK.
WHY?
© 1994 Washington Post Writers Group
SO THAT SOMEDAY YOU'LL BE ABLE TO GET A GOOD JOB.
WHY?
SO YOU CAN WORK YOUR TAIL OFF FOR THIRTY OR FORTY YEARS AND THEN RETIRE.
WHY?
4·19
BRIAN CRANE
SO YOU CAN WATCH TV.

PICKLES

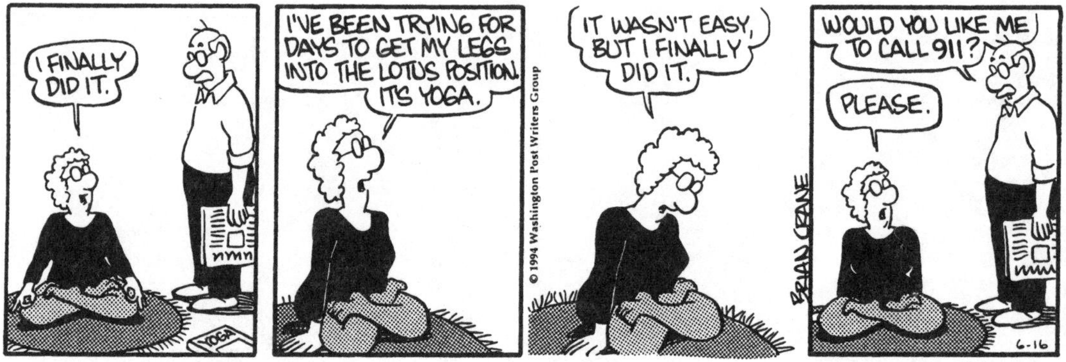
I FINALLY DID IT.
I'VE BEEN TRYING FOR DAYS TO GET MY LEGS INTO THE LOTUS POSITION.
IT'S YOGA.
© 1994 Washington Post Writers Group
IT WASN'T EASY, BUT I FINALLY DID IT.
WOULD YOU LIKE ME TO CALL 911?
PLEASE.
YOGA
BRIAN CRANE
6-16

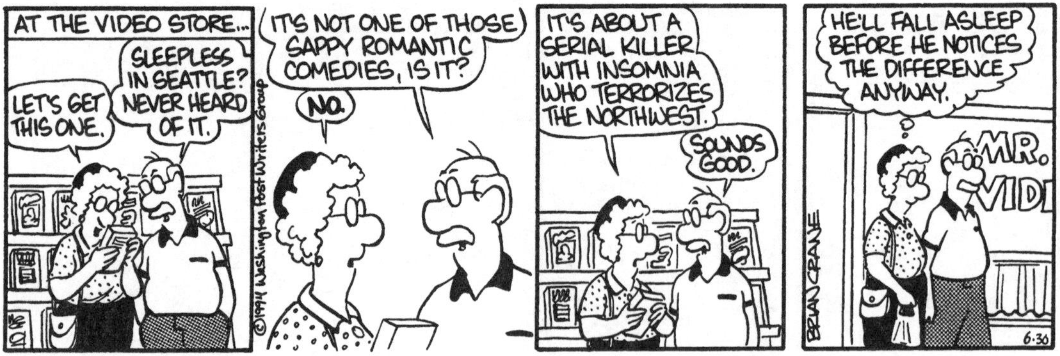
AT THE VIDEO STORE...
LET'S GET THIS ONE.
SLEEPLESS IN SEATTLE? NEVER HEARD OF IT.
©1994 Washington Post Writers Group
IT'S NOT ONE OF THOSE SAPPY ROMANTIC COMEDIES, IS IT?
NO.
IT'S ABOUT A SERIAL KILLER WITH INSOMNIA WHO TERRORIZES THE NORTHWEST.
SOUNDS GOOD.
HE'LL FALL ASLEEP BEFORE HE NOTICES THE DIFFERENCE ANYWAY.
MR. VID
BRIAN CRANE
6-30

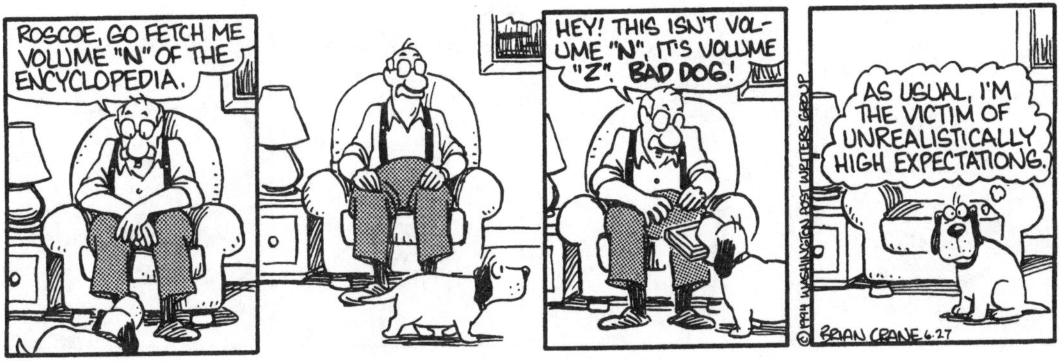
ROSCOE, GO FETCH ME VOLUME "N" OF THE ENCYCLOPEDIA.
HEY! THIS ISN'T VOLUME "N", IT'S VOLUME "Z". BAD DOG!
AS USUAL, I'M THE VICTIM OF UNREALISTICALLY HIGH EXPECTATIONS.
© 1994 WASHINGTON POST WRITERS GROUP
BRIAN CRANE 6.27

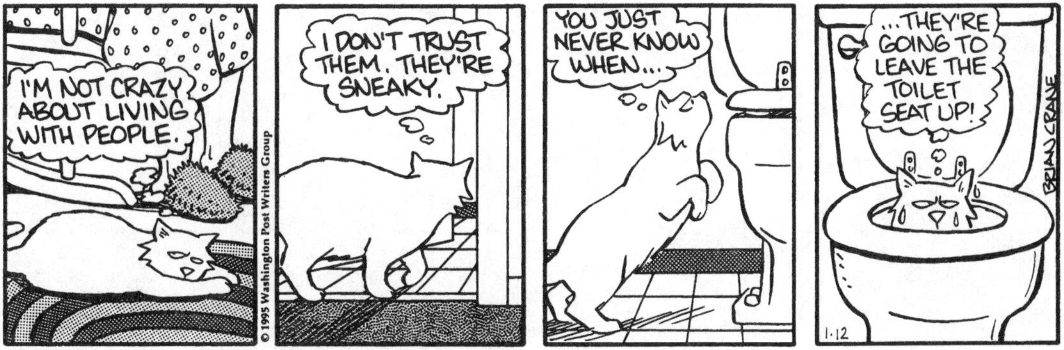
I'M NOT CRAZY ABOUT LIVING WITH PEOPLE.
© 1995 Washington Post Writers Group
I DON'T TRUST THEM. THEY'RE SNEAKY.
YOU JUST NEVER KNOW WHEN...
...THEY'RE GOING TO LEAVE THE TOILET SEAT UP!
BRIAN CRANE
1.12

PICKLES

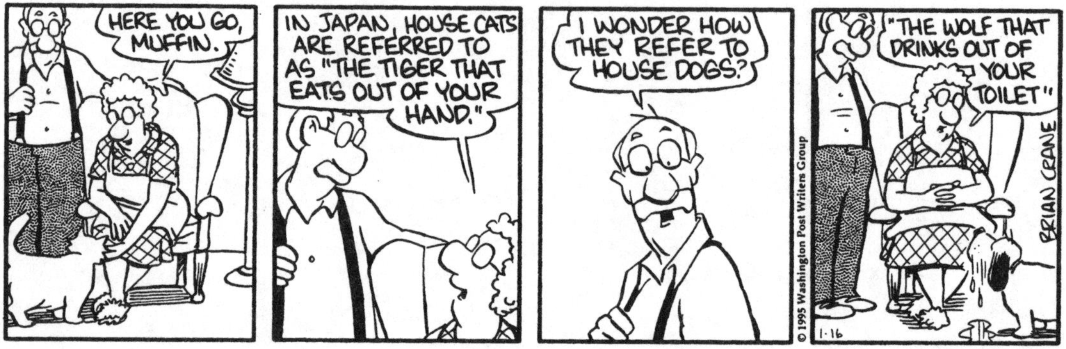
HERE YOU GO, MUFFIN.
IN JAPAN, HOUSE CATS ARE REFERRED TO AS "THE TIGER THAT EATS OUT OF YOUR HAND."
I WONDER HOW THEY REFER TO HOUSE DOGS?
"THE WOLF THAT DRINKS OUT OF YOUR TOILET"
© 1995 Washington Post Writers Group
1·16
BRIAN CRANE

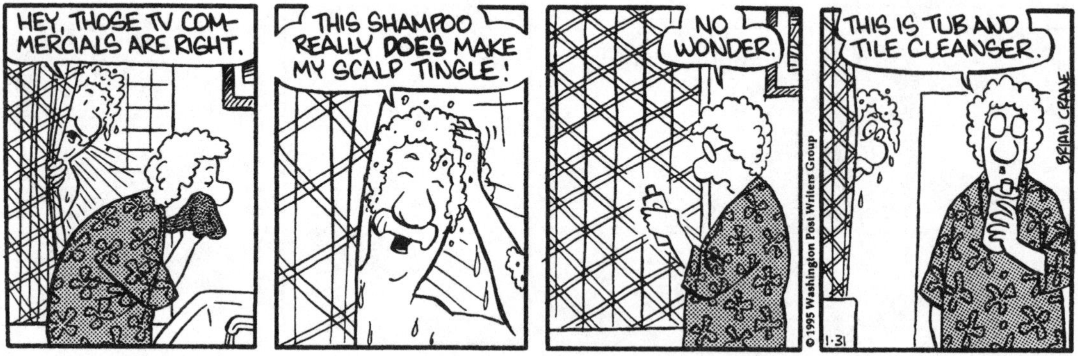
HEY, THOSE TV COMMERCIALS ARE RIGHT.
THIS SHAMPOO REALLY **DOES** MAKE MY SCALP TINGLE!
NO WONDER.
THIS IS TUB AND TILE CLEANSER.
© 1995 Washington Post Writers Group
1·31
BRIAN CRANE

PICKLES

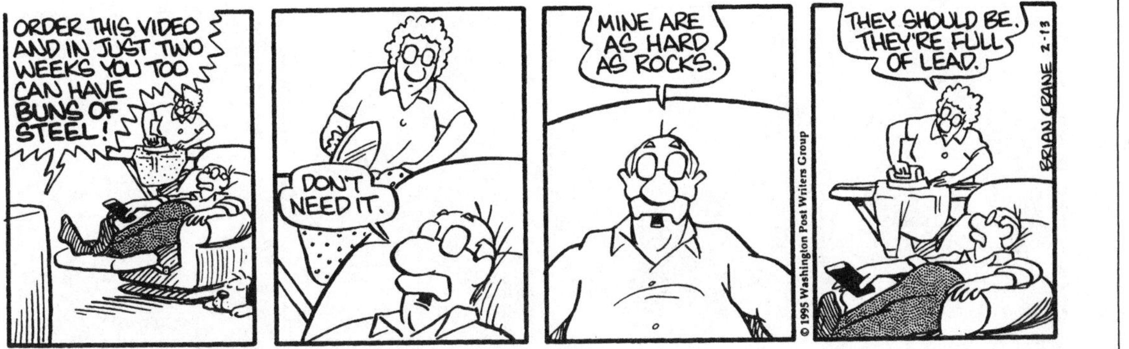
ORDER THIS VIDEO AND IN JUST TWO WEEKS YOU TOO CAN HAVE BUNS OF STEEL!
DON'T NEED IT.
MINE ARE AS HARD AS ROCKS.
THEY SHOULD BE. THEY'RE FULL OF LEAD.
© 1995 Washington Post Writers Group
BRIAN CRANE 2-13

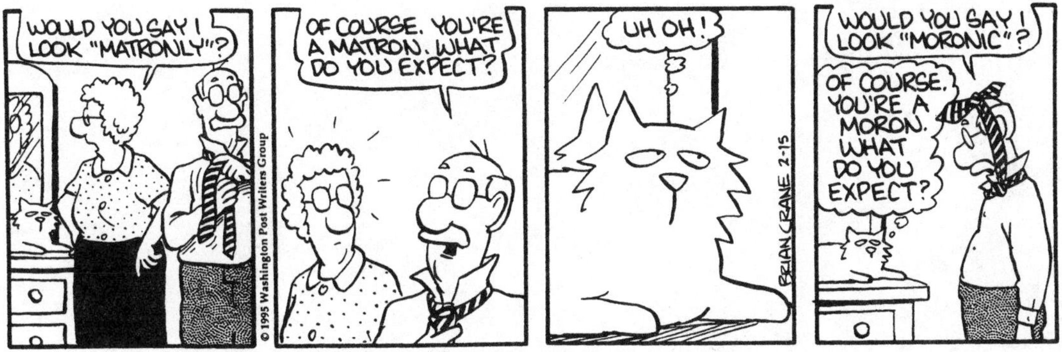
WOULD YOU SAY I LOOK "MATRONLY"?
© 1995 Washington Post Writers Group
OF COURSE. YOU'RE A MATRON. WHAT DO YOU EXPECT?
UH OH!
BRIAN CRANE 2-15
WOULD YOU SAY I LOOK "MORONIC"?
OF COURSE. YOU'RE A MORON. WHAT DO YOU EXPECT?

PICKLES

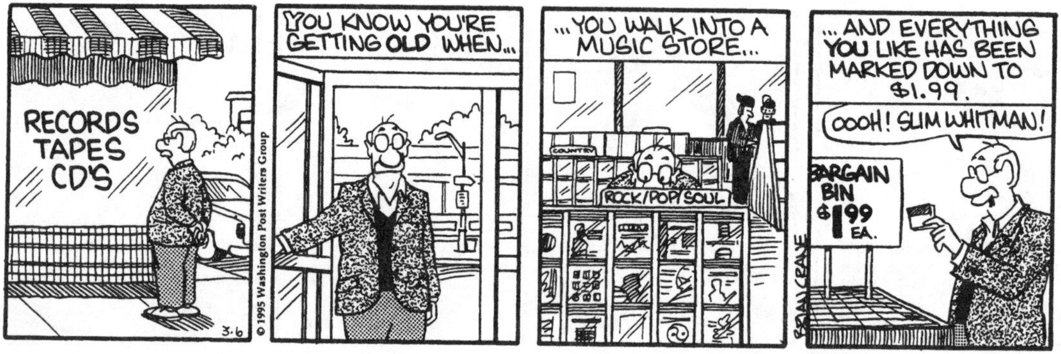
RECORDS
TAPES
CD'S
3-6
© 1995 Washington Post Writers Group
YOU KNOW YOU'RE GETTING OLD WHEN...
...YOU WALK INTO A MUSIC STORE...
COUNTRY
ROCK/POP/SOUL
BRIAN CRANE
...AND EVERYTHING YOU LIKE HAS BEEN MARKED DOWN TO $1.99.
OOOH! SLIM WHITMAN!
BARGAIN BIN $1.99 EA.

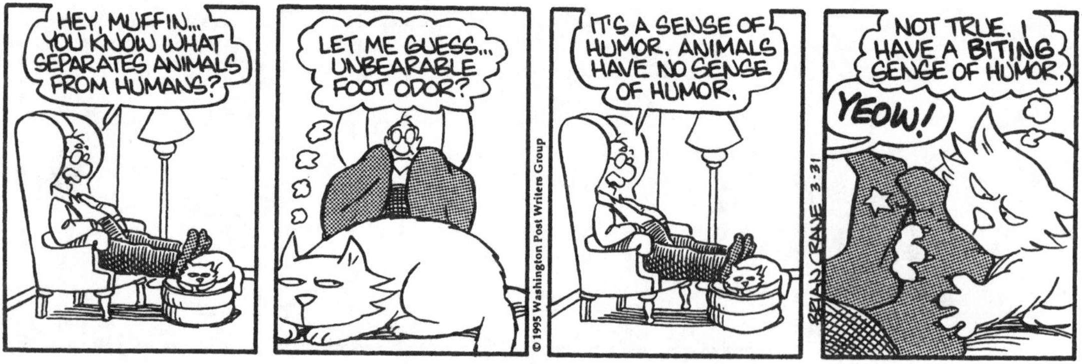
HEY, MUFFIN... YOU KNOW WHAT SEPARATES ANIMALS FROM HUMANS?
LET ME GUESS... UNBEARABLE FOOT ODOR?
© 1995 Washington Post Writers Group
IT'S A SENSE OF HUMOR. ANIMALS HAVE NO SENSE OF HUMOR.
BRIAN CRANE 3-31
NOT TRUE. I HAVE A BITING SENSE OF HUMOR.
YEOW!

PICKLES

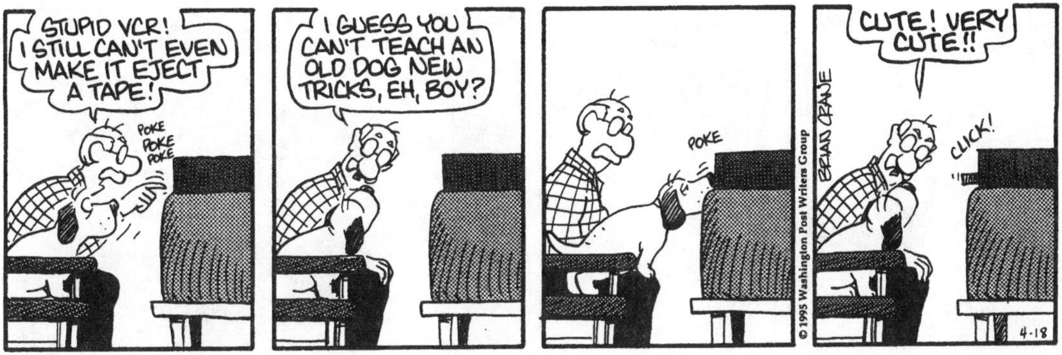
STUPID VCR! I STILL CAN'T EVEN MAKE IT EJECT A TAPE!
POKE POKE POKE
I GUESS YOU CAN'T TEACH AN OLD DOG NEW TRICKS, EH, BOY?
POKE
© 1995 Washington Post Writers Group
BRIAN CRANE
CUTE! VERY CUTE!!
CLICK!
4-18

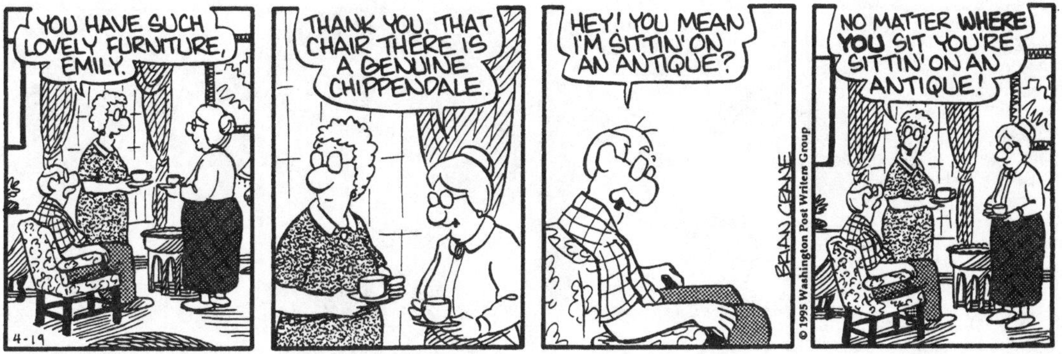
YOU HAVE SUCH LOVELY FURNITURE, EMILY.
4-19
THANK YOU. THAT CHAIR THERE IS A GENUINE CHIPPENDALE.
HEY! YOU MEAN I'M SITTIN' ON AN ANTIQUE?
BRIAN CRANE
© 1995 Washington Post Writers Group
NO MATTER **WHERE YOU** SIT YOU'RE SITTIN' ON AN ANTIQUE!

PICKLES

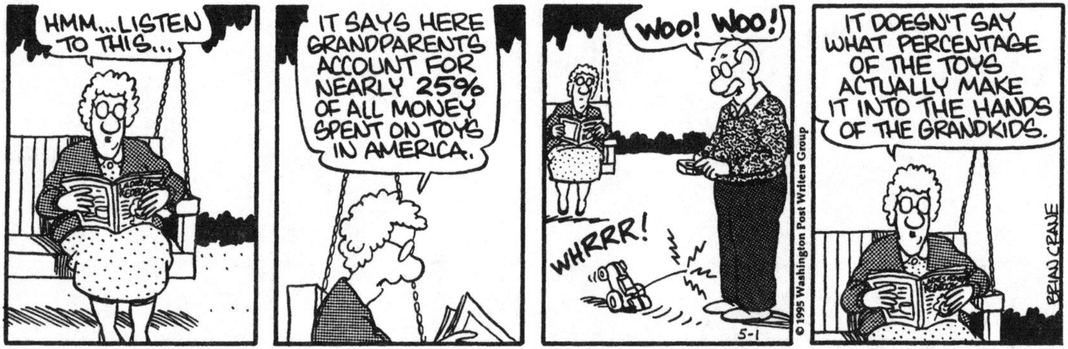
HMM...LISTEN TO THIS...
IT SAYS HERE GRANDPARENTS ACCOUNT FOR NEARLY 25% OF ALL MONEY SPENT ON TOYS IN AMERICA.
WOO! WOO!
WHRRR!
IT DOESN'T SAY WHAT PERCENTAGE OF THE TOYS ACTUALLY MAKE IT INTO THE HANDS OF THE GRANDKIDS.
5-1
© 1995 Washington Post Writers Group
BRIAN CRANE

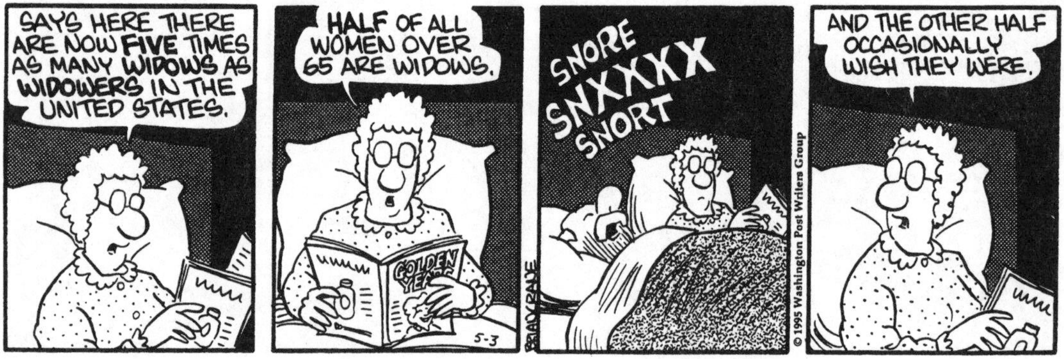
SAYS HERE THERE ARE NOW **FIVE** TIMES AS MANY **WIDOWS** AS **WIDOWERS** IN THE UNITED STATES.
HALF OF ALL WOMEN OVER 65 ARE WIDOWS.
GOLDEN YEARS
SNORE
SNXXXX
SNORT
AND THE OTHER HALF OCCASIONALLY WISH THEY WERE.
5-3
BRIAN CRANE
© 1995 Washington Post Writers Group

PICKLES

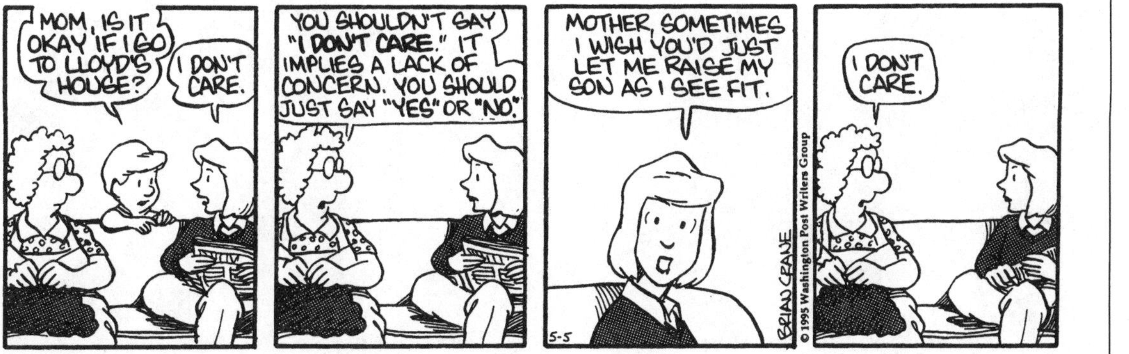
MOM, IS IT OKAY IF I GO TO LLOYD'S HOUSE?
I DON'T CARE.
YOU SHOULDN'T SAY "I DON'T CARE." IT IMPLIES A LACK OF CONCERN. YOU SHOULD JUST SAY "YES" OR "NO."
MOTHER, SOMETIMES I WISH YOU'D JUST LET ME RAISE MY SON AS I SEE FIT.
5-5
BRIAN CRANE
© 1995 Washington Post Writers Group
I DON'T CARE.

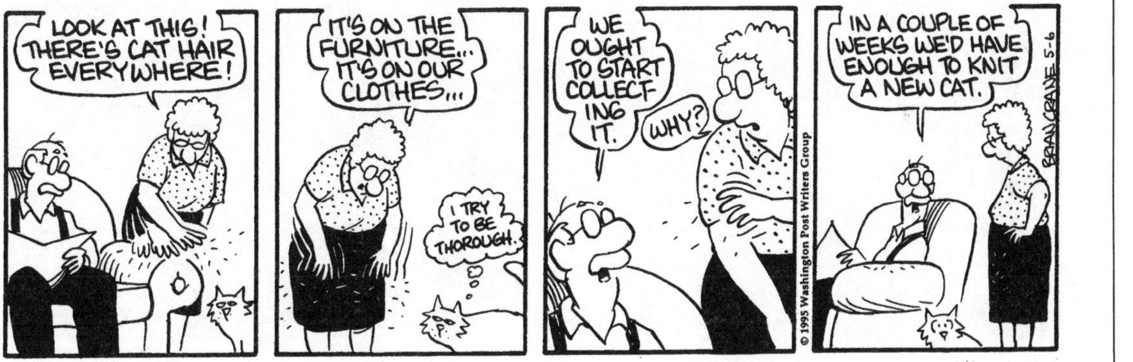
LOOK AT THIS! THERE'S CAT HAIR EVERYWHERE!
IT'S ON THE FURNITURE... IT'S ON OUR CLOTHES...
I TRY TO BE THOROUGH.
WE OUGHT TO START COLLECT-ING IT.
WHY?
© 1995 Washington Post Writers Group
IN A COUPLE OF WEEKS WE'D HAVE ENOUGH TO KNIT A NEW CAT.
BRIAN CRANE 5-6

PICKLES

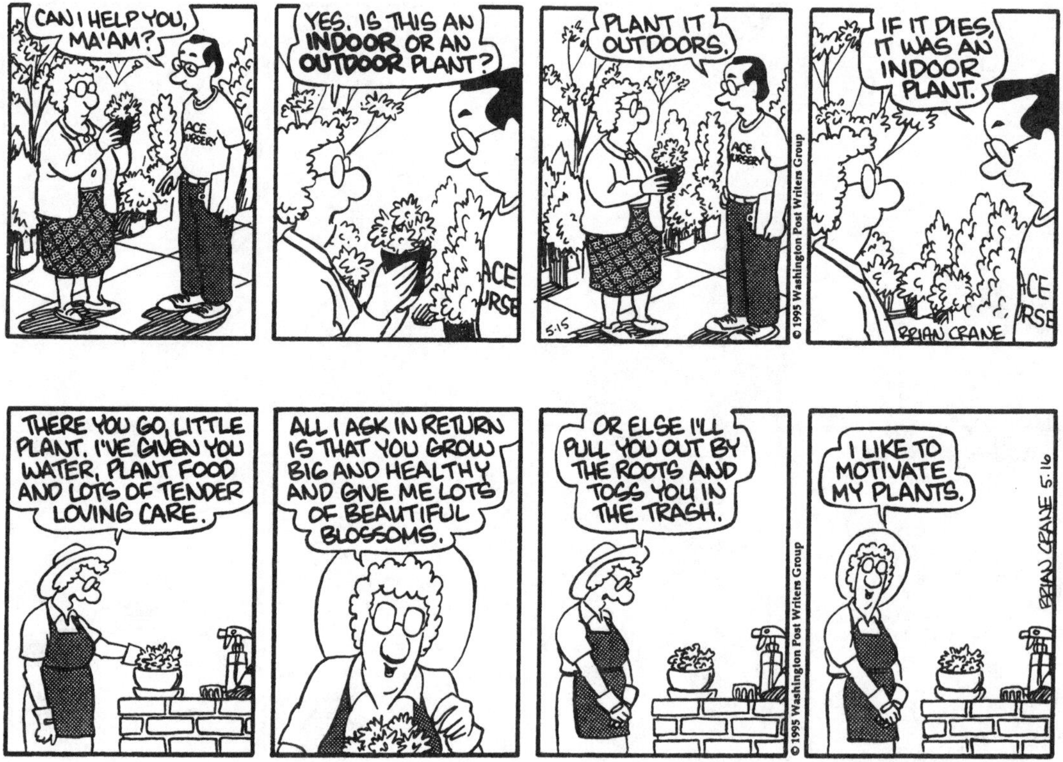

CAN I HELP YOU, MA'AM?
ACE NURSERY
YES. IS THIS AN INDOOR OR AN OUTDOOR PLANT?
PLANT IT OUTDOORS.
5-15
© 1995 Washington Post Writers Group
IF IT DIES, IT WAS AN INDOOR PLANT.
BRIAN CRANE
THERE YOU GO, LITTLE PLANT. I'VE GIVEN YOU WATER, PLANT FOOD AND LOTS OF TENDER LOVING CARE.
ALL I ASK IN RETURN IS THAT YOU GROW BIG AND HEALTHY AND GIVE ME LOTS OF BEAUTIFUL BLOSSOMS.
OR ELSE I'LL PULL YOU OUT BY THE ROOTS AND TOSS YOU IN THE TRASH.
© 1995 Washington Post Writers Group
I LIKE TO MOTIVATE MY PLANTS.
BRIAN CRANE 5-16

PICKLES

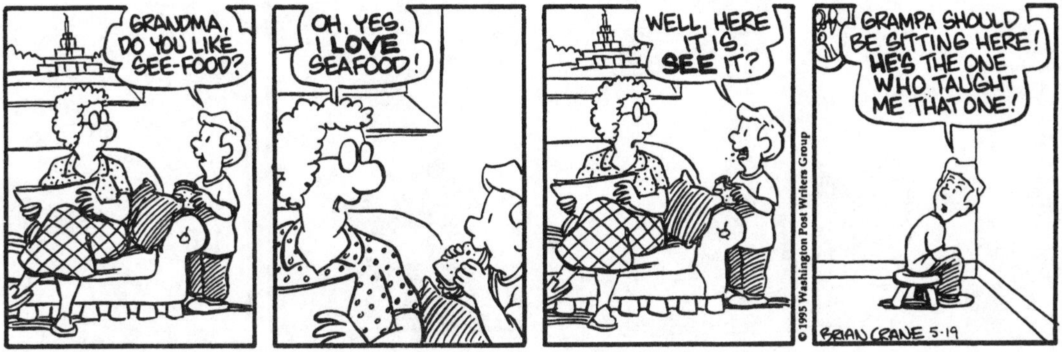
GRANDMA, DO YOU LIKE SEE-FOOD?
OH, YES. I LOVE SEAFOOD!
WELL, HERE IT IS. SEE IT?
© 1995 Washington Post Writers Group
GRAMPA SHOULD BE SITTING HERE! HE'S THE ONE WHO TAUGHT ME THAT ONE!
BRIAN CRANE 5-19

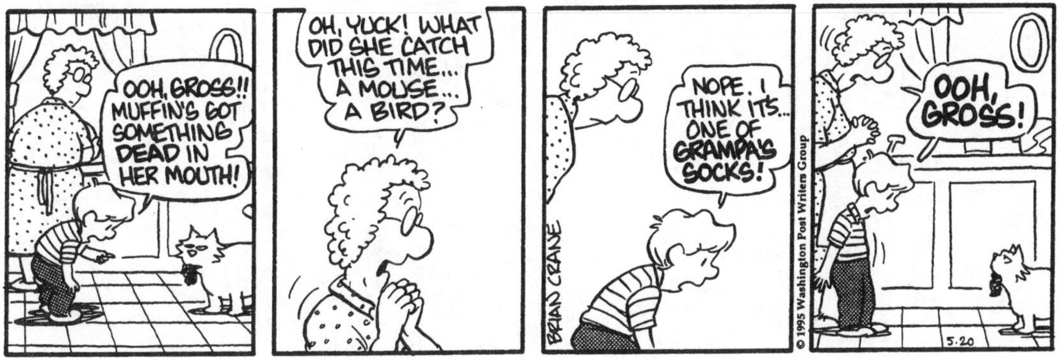
OOH, GROSS!! MUFFIN'S GOT SOMETHING DEAD IN HER MOUTH!
OH, YUCK! WHAT DID SHE CATCH THIS TIME... A MOUSE... A BIRD?
BRIAN CRANE
NOPE. I THINK IT'S... ONE OF GRAMPA'S SOCKS!
© 1995 Washington Post Writers Group
OOH, GROSS!
5-20

PICKLES

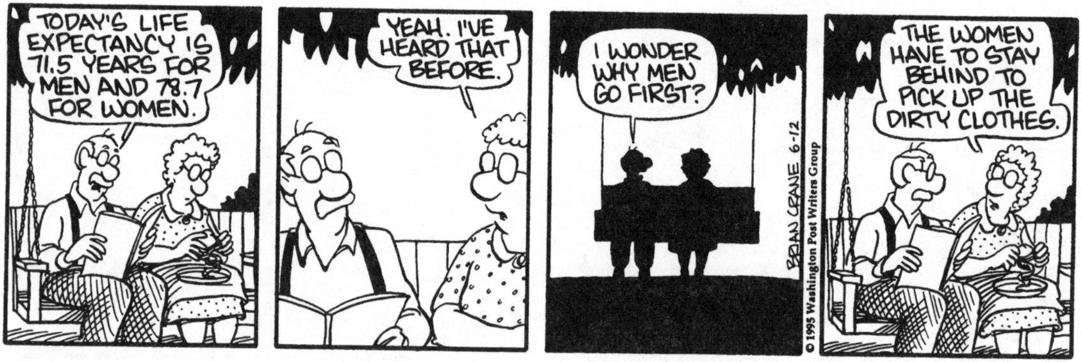

TODAY'S LIFE EXPECTANCY IS 71.5 YEARS FOR MEN AND 78.7 FOR WOMEN.
YEAH. I'VE HEARD THAT BEFORE.
I WONDER WHY MEN GO FIRST?
BRIAN CRANE 6-12
© 1995 Washington Post Writers Group
THE WOMEN HAVE TO STAY BEHIND TO PICK UP THE DIRTY CLOTHES.

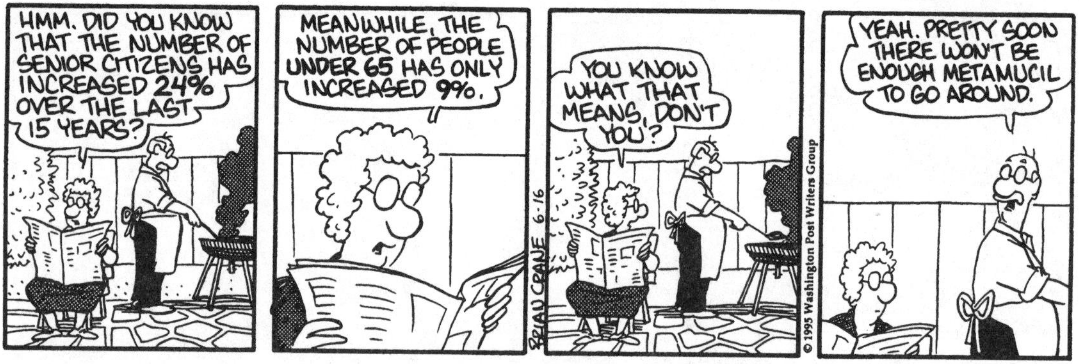

HMM. DID YOU KNOW THAT THE NUMBER OF SENIOR CITIZENS HAS INCREASED 24% OVER THE LAST 15 YEARS?
MEANWHILE, THE NUMBER OF PEOPLE UNDER 65 HAS ONLY INCREASED 9%.
BRIAN CRANE 6-16
YOU KNOW WHAT THAT MEANS, DON'T YOU?
© 1995 Washington Post Writers Group
YEAH. PRETTY SOON THERE WON'T BE ENOUGH METAMUCIL TO GO AROUND.

PICKLES

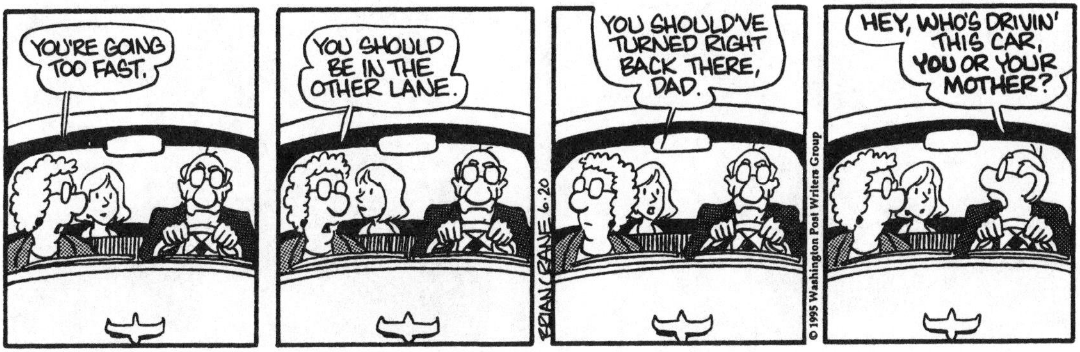

YOU'RE GOING TOO FAST.
YOU SHOULD BE IN THE OTHER LANE.
BRIAN CRANE 6·20
YOU SHOULD'VE TURNED RIGHT BACK THERE, DAD.
© 1995 Washington Post Writers Group
HEY, WHO'S DRIVIN' THIS CAR, YOU OR YOUR MOTHER?

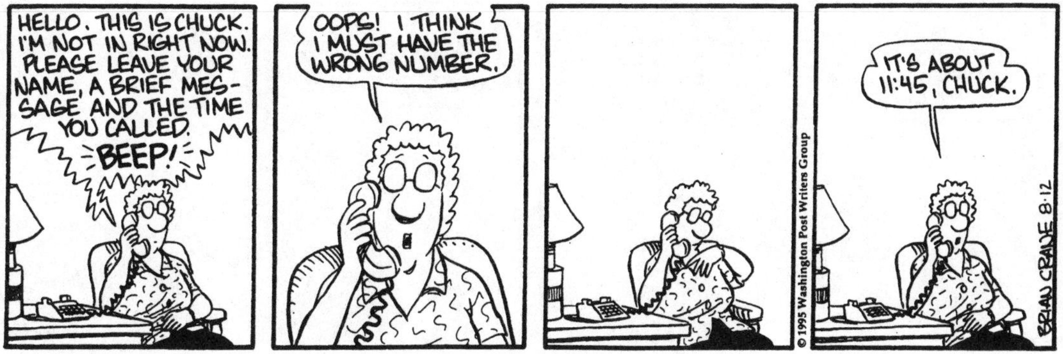

HELLO. THIS IS CHUCK. I'M NOT IN RIGHT NOW. PLEASE LEAVE YOUR NAME, A BRIEF MES-SAGE AND THE TIME YOU CALLED.
BEEP!
OOPS! I THINK I MUST HAVE THE WRONG NUMBER.
© 1995 Washington Post Writers Group
IT'S ABOUT 11:45, CHUCK.
BRIAN CRANE 8·12

PICKLES

HOW MUCH FOR THE LEISURE SUIT?
GARAGE SALE
TWO BUCKS.
I'LL GIVE YOU A DOLLAR FOR IT.
TWO BUCKS. TAKE IT OR LEAVE IT.
BRIAN CRANE 6·26
TWO BUCKS, HUH?
© 1995 Washington Post Writers Group
WELL, OKAY. I GUESS IF YOU WANT QUALITY MERCHANDISE YOU'VE GOT TO BE PREPARED TO PAY FOR IT.
JINGLE JINGLE

YOU KNOW, THE WORLD WOULD BE A MUCH BETTER PLACE IF EVERYONE WORE LEISURE SUITS.
I THINK IT'S ALL THOSE SUSPENDERS, BELTS AND NECKTIES THAT MAKE EVERYONE SO CRANKY.
EARL! ARE YOU GOING TO SIT ON YOUR DUFF ALL DAY, OR GET UP AND DO SOMETHING?!
© 1995 Washington Post Writers Group
GIRDLES AND PANTY HOSE'LL DO IT TOO.
BRIAN CRANE 6·28

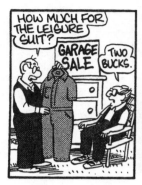

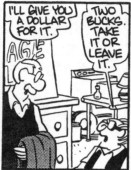

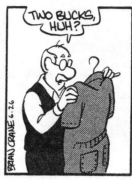

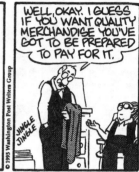

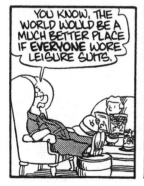

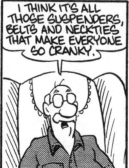

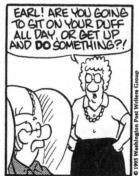

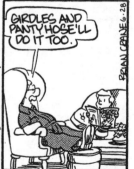

PICKLES

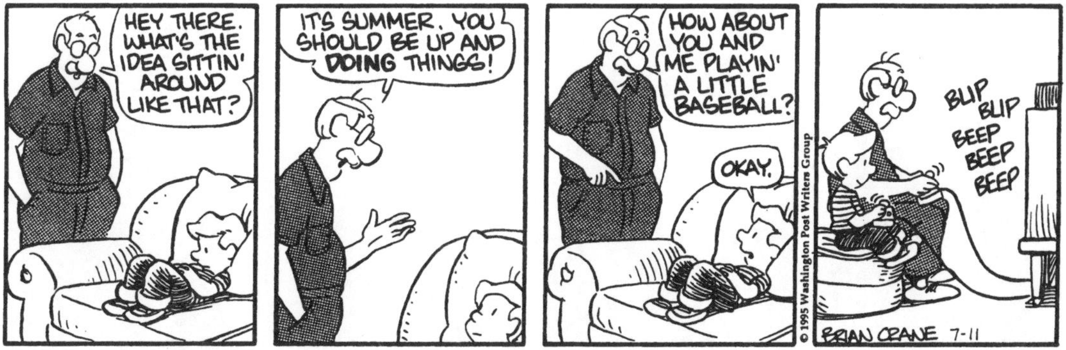
HEY THERE. WHAT'S THE IDEA SITTIN' AROUND LIKE THAT?
IT'S SUMMER. YOU SHOULD BE UP AND DOING THINGS!
HOW ABOUT YOU AND ME PLAYIN' A LITTLE BASEBALL?
OKAY.
BLIP BLIP BEEP BEEP BEEP
© 1995 Washington Post Writers Group
BRIAN CRANE 7-11

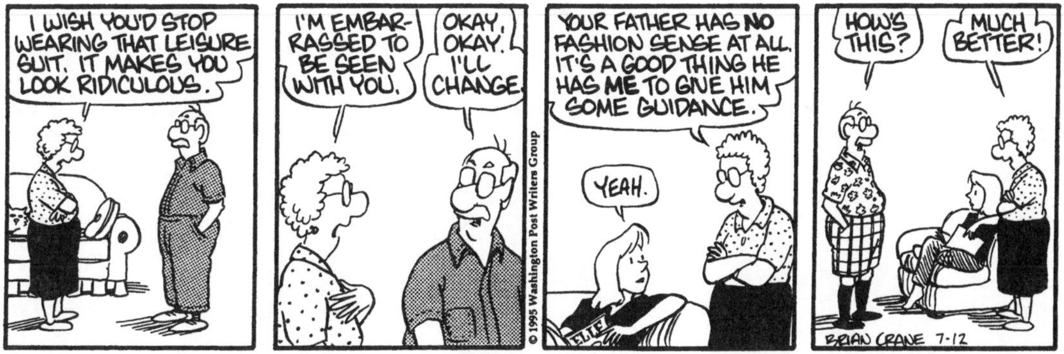
I WISH YOU'D STOP WEARING THAT LEISURE SUIT. IT MAKES YOU LOOK RIDICULOUS.
I'M EMBARRASSED TO BE SEEN WITH YOU.
OKAY, OKAY. I'LL CHANGE.
© 1995 Washington Post Writers Group
YOUR FATHER HAS NO FASHION SENSE AT ALL. IT'S A GOOD THING HE HAS ME TO GIVE HIM SOME GUIDANCE.
YEAH.
ELLE
HOW'S THIS?
MUCH BETTER!
BRIAN CRANE 7-12

PICKLES

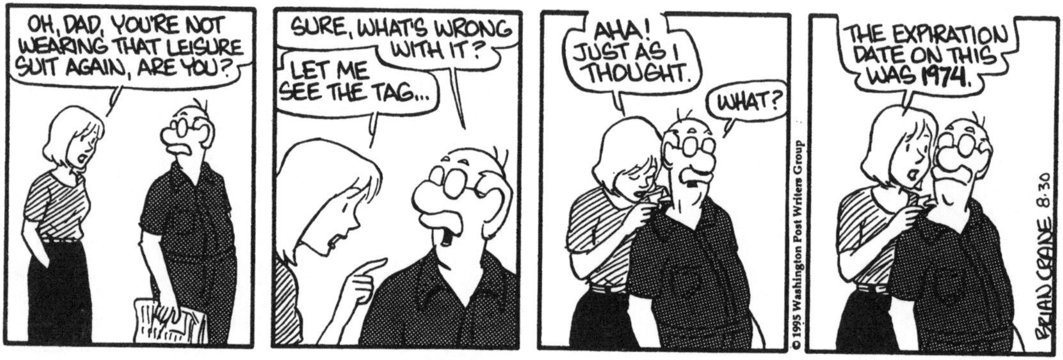
OH, DAD, YOU'RE NOT WEARING THAT LEISURE SUIT AGAIN, ARE YOU?
SURE, WHAT'S WRONG WITH IT?
LET ME SEE THE TAG...
AHA! JUST AS I THOUGHT.
WHAT?
THE EXPIRATION DATE ON THIS WAS 1974.
© 1995 Washington Post Writers Group
BRIAN CRANE 8-30

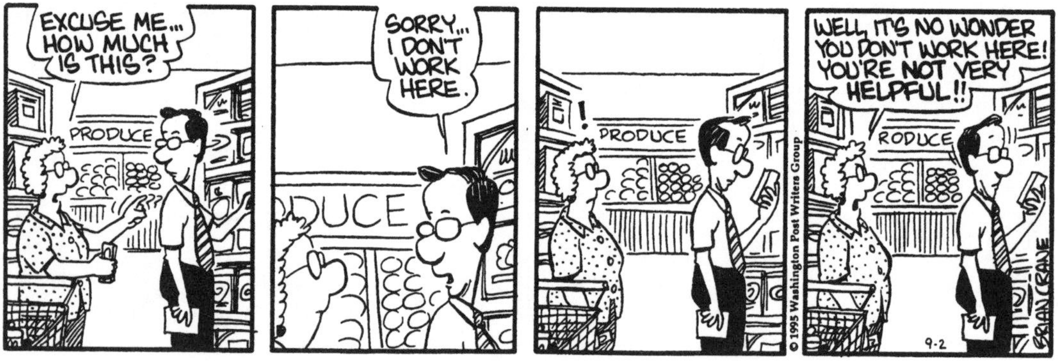
EXCUSE ME... HOW MUCH IS THIS?
PRODUCE
SORRY... I DON'T WORK HERE.
!
WELL, IT'S NO WONDER YOU DON'T WORK HERE! YOU'RE NOT VERY HELPFUL!!
© 1995 Washington Post Writers Group
9-2
BRIAN CRANE

PICKLES

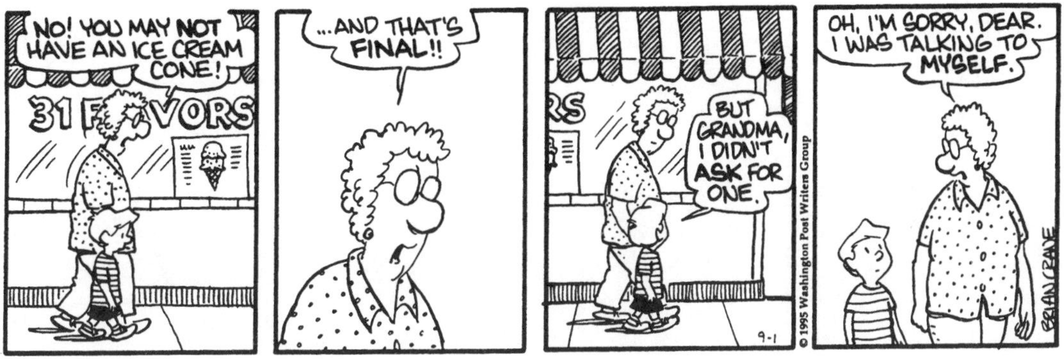
NO! YOU MAY NOT HAVE AN ICE CREAM CONE!
31 F VORS
...AND THAT'S FINAL!!
BUT GRANDMA, I DIDN'T ASK FOR ONE.
© 1995 Washington Post Writers Group
9-1
OH, I'M SORRY, DEAR. I WAS TALKING TO MYSELF.
BRIAN CRANE

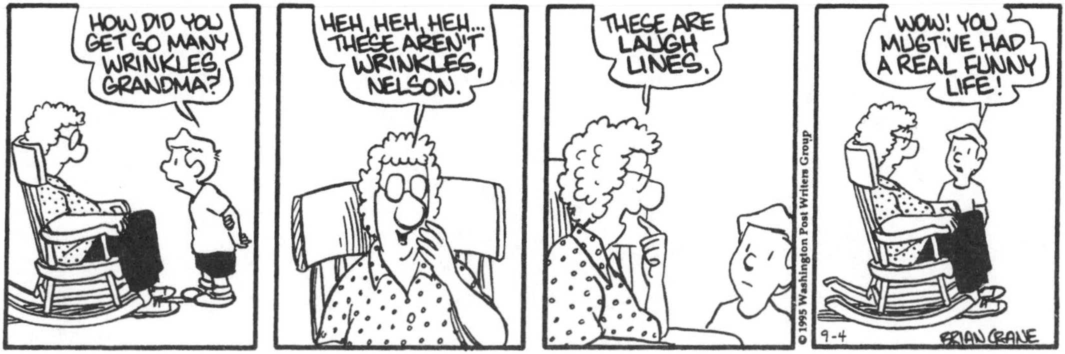
HOW DID YOU GET SO MANY WRINKLES, GRANDMA?
HEH, HEH, HEH... THESE AREN'T WRINKLES, NELSON.
THESE ARE LAUGH LINES.
© 1995 Washington Post Writers Group
WOW! YOU MUST'VE HAD A REAL FUNNY LIFE!
9-4
BRIAN CRANE

PICKLES

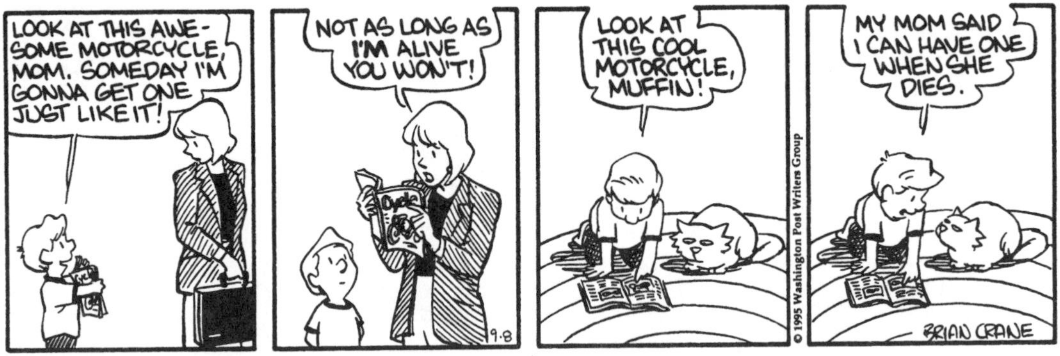
LOOK AT THIS AWESOME MOTORCYCLE, MOM. SOMEDAY I'M GONNA GET ONE JUST LIKE IT!
NOT AS LONG AS I'M ALIVE YOU WON'T!
9.8
LOOK AT THIS COOL MOTORCYCLE, MUFFIN!
© 1995 Washington Post Writers Group
MY MOM SAID I CAN HAVE ONE WHEN SHE DIES.
BRIAN CRANE

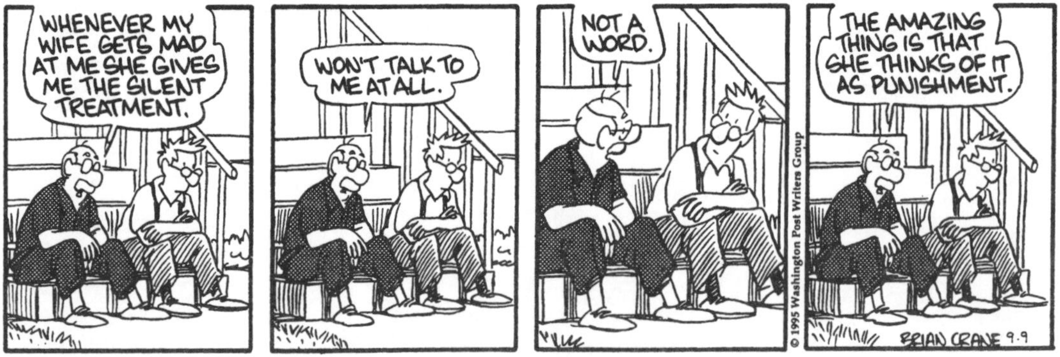
WHENEVER MY WIFE GETS MAD AT ME SHE GIVES ME THE SILENT TREATMENT.
WON'T TALK TO ME AT ALL.
NOT A WORD.
© 1995 Washington Post Writers Group
THE AMAZING THING IS THAT SHE THINKS OF IT AS PUNISHMENT.
BRIAN CRANE 9.9

PICKLES

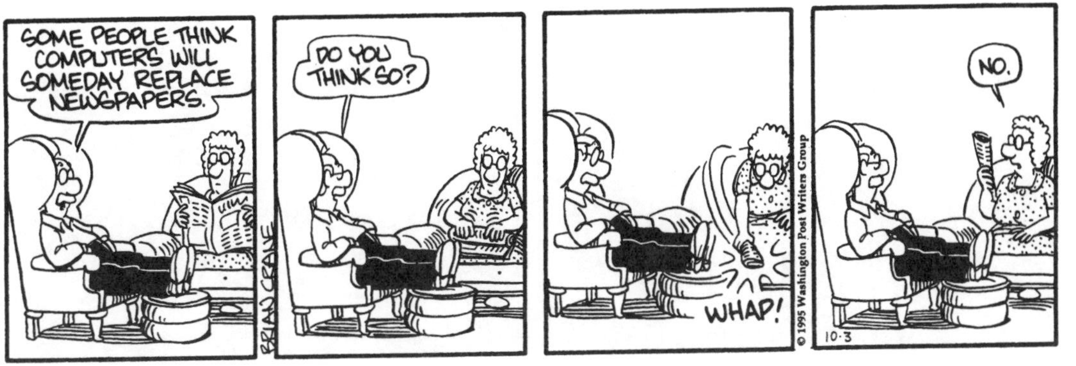
SOME PEOPLE THINK COMPUTERS WILL SOMEDAY REPLACE NEWSPAPERS.
BRIAN CRANE
DO YOU THINK SO?
WHAP!
© 1995 Washington Post Writers Group
NO.
10·3

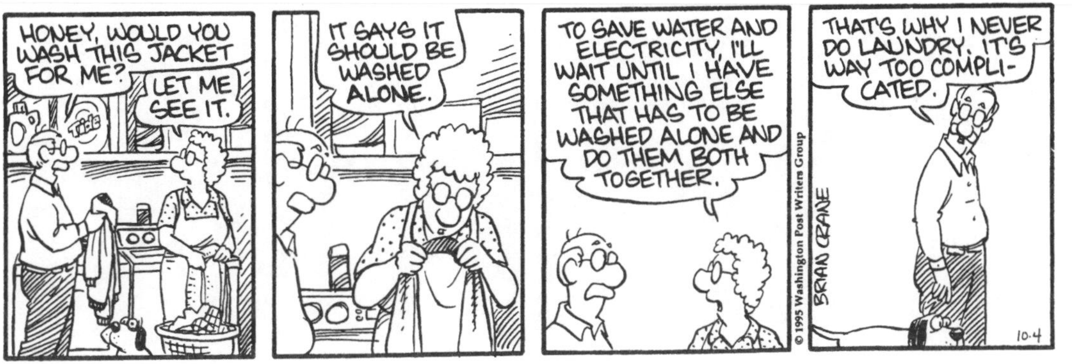
HONEY, WOULD YOU WASH THIS JACKET FOR ME?
LET ME SEE IT.
TIDE
IT SAYS IT SHOULD BE WASHED ALONE.
TO SAVE WATER AND ELECTRICITY, I'LL WAIT UNTIL I HAVE SOMETHING ELSE THAT HAS TO BE WASHED ALONE AND DO THEM BOTH TOGETHER.
© 1995 Washington Post Writers Group
BRIAN CRANE
THAT'S WHY I NEVER DO LAUNDRY. IT'S WAY TOO COMPLICATED.
10·4

PICKLES

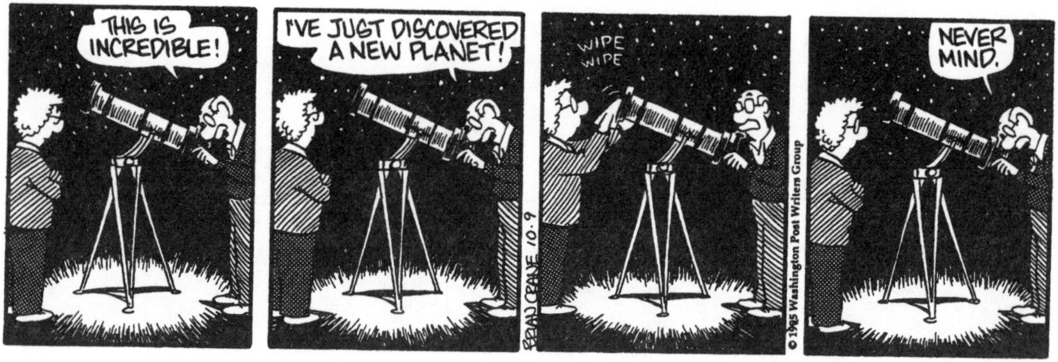
THIS IS INCREDIBLE!
I'VE JUST DISCOVERED A NEW PLANET!
WIPE WIPE
NEVER MIND.
BRIAN CRANE 10·9
© 1995 Washington Post Writers Group

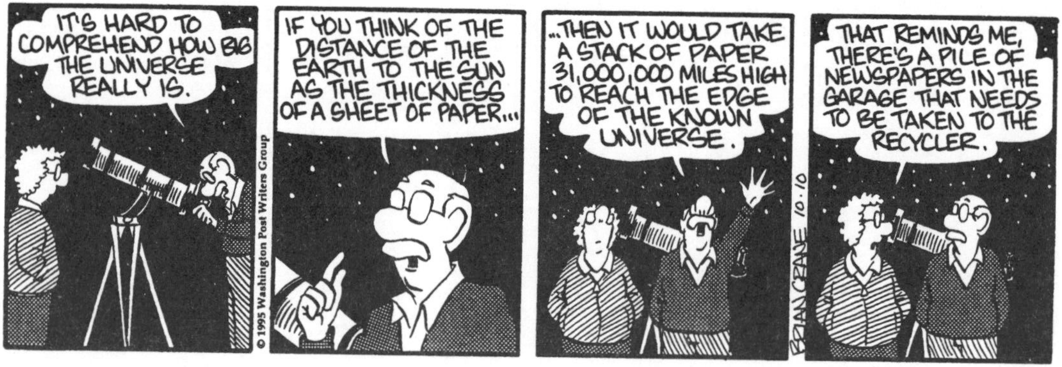
IT'S HARD TO COMPREHEND HOW BIG THE UNIVERSE REALLY IS.
© 1995 Washington Post Writers Group
IF YOU THINK OF THE DISTANCE OF THE EARTH TO THE SUN AS THE THICKNESS OF A SHEET OF PAPER...
...THEN IT WOULD TAKE A STACK OF PAPER 31,000,000 MILES HIGH TO REACH THE EDGE OF THE KNOWN UNIVERSE.
BRIAN CRANE 10·10
THAT REMINDS ME, THERE'S A PILE OF NEWSPAPERS IN THE GARAGE THAT NEEDS TO BE TAKEN TO THE RECYCLER.

PICKLES

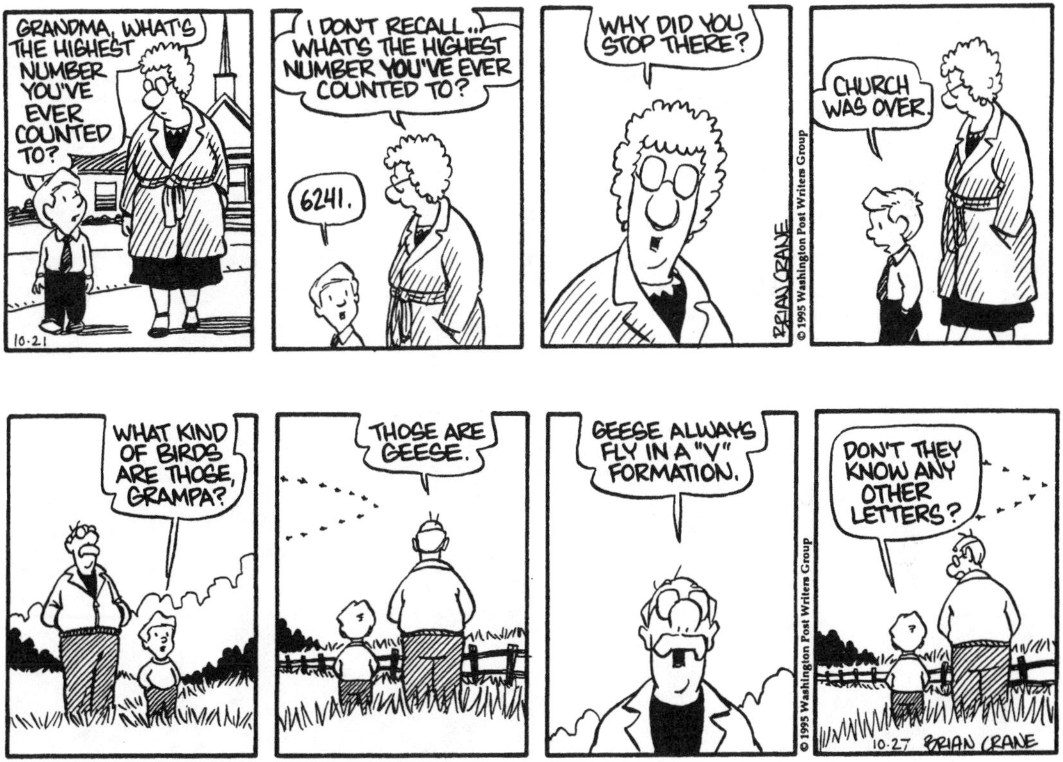
GRANDMA, WHAT'S THE HIGHEST NUMBER YOU'VE EVER COUNTED TO?
10·21
I DON'T RECALL... WHAT'S THE HIGHEST NUMBER YOU'VE EVER COUNTED TO?
6241.
WHY DID YOU STOP THERE?
BRIAN CRANE
© 1995 Washington Post Writers Group
CHURCH WAS OVER.
WHAT KIND OF BIRDS ARE THOSE, GRAMPA?
THOSE ARE GEESE.
GEESE ALWAYS FLY IN A "V" FORMATION.
© 1995 Washington Post Writers Group
DON'T THEY KNOW ANY OTHER LETTERS?
10·27 BRIAN CRANE

PICKLES

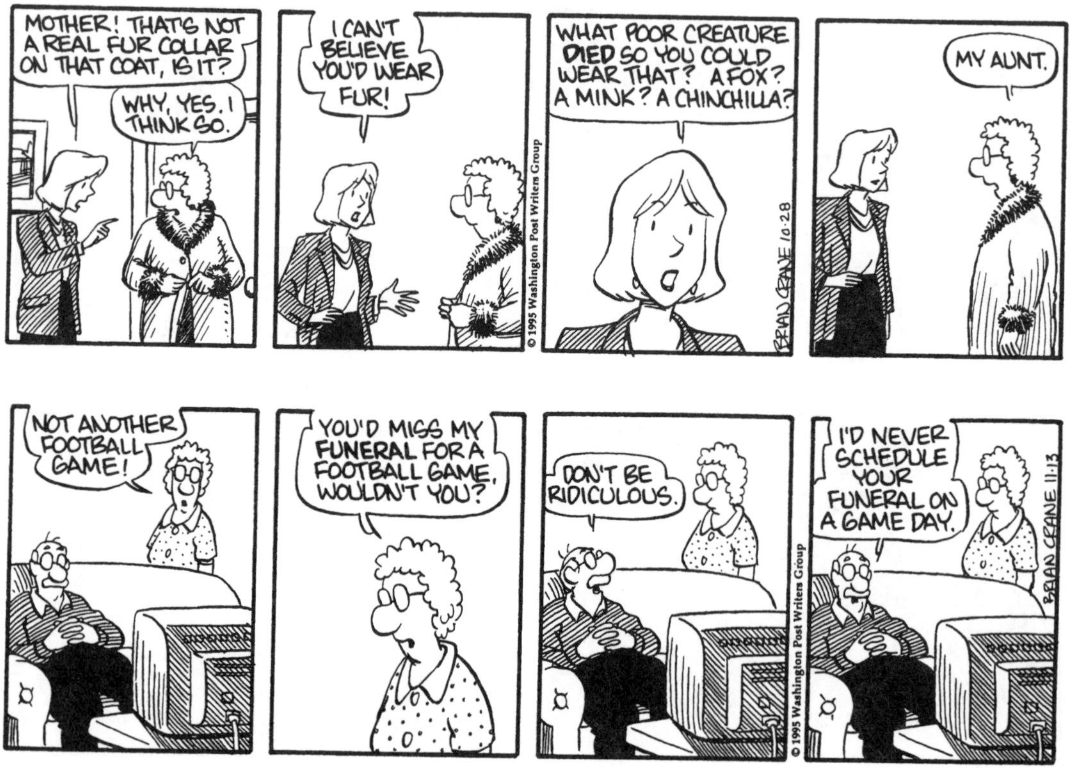

MOTHER! THAT'S NOT A REAL FUR COLLAR ON THAT COAT, IS IT?
WHY, YES. I THINK SO.
I CAN'T BELIEVE YOU'D WEAR FUR!
WHAT POOR CREATURE DIED SO YOU COULD WEAR THAT? A FOX? A MINK? A CHINCHILLA?
MY AUNT.
© 1995 Washington Post Writers Group
BRIAN CRANE 10·28
NOT ANOTHER FOOTBALL GAME!
YOU'D MISS MY FUNERAL FOR A FOOTBALL GAME, WOULDN'T YOU?
DON'T BE RIDICULOUS.
I'D NEVER SCHEDULE YOUR FUNERAL ON A GAME DAY.
© 1995 Washington Post Writers Group
BRIAN CRANE 11·13

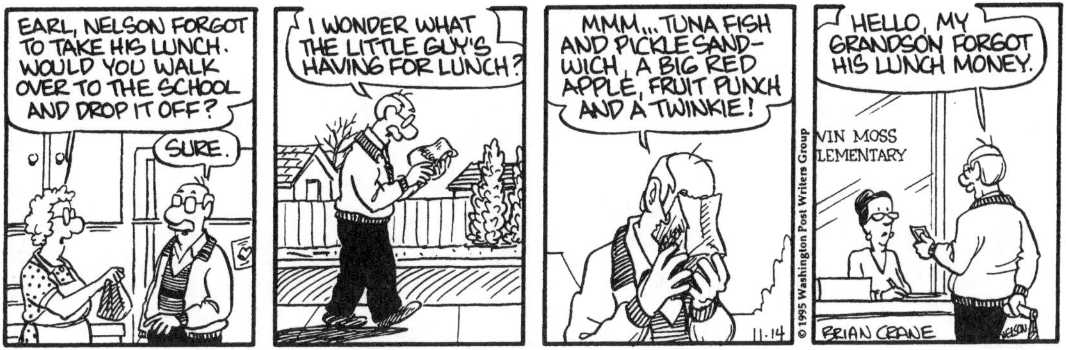
EARL, NELSON FORGOT TO TAKE HIS LUNCH. WOULD YOU WALK OVER TO THE SCHOOL AND DROP IT OFF?
SURE.
I WONDER WHAT THE LITTLE GUY'S HAVING FOR LUNCH?
MMM... TUNA FISH AND PICKLE SANDWICH, A BIG RED APPLE, FRUIT PUNCH AND A TWINKIE!
11-14
© 1995 Washington Post Writers Group
VIN MOSS
LEMENTARY
HELLO, MY GRANDSON FORGOT HIS LUNCH MONEY.
NELSON
BRIAN CRANE

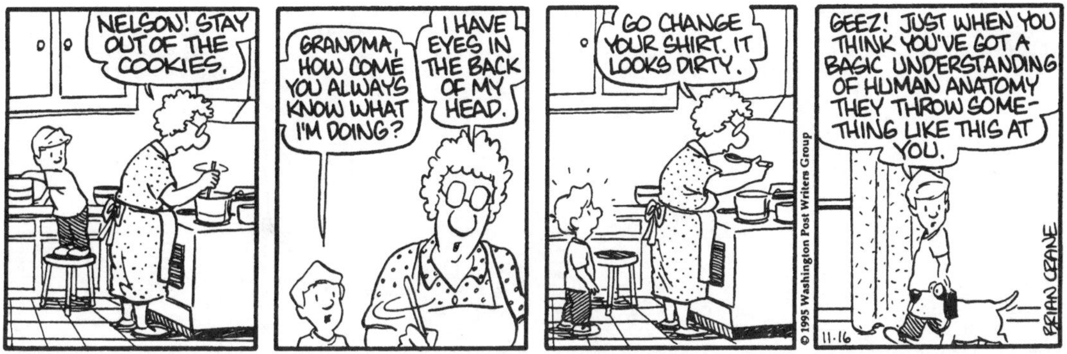
NELSON! STAY OUT OF THE COOKIES.
GRANDMA, HOW COME YOU ALWAYS KNOW WHAT I'M DOING?
I HAVE EYES IN THE BACK OF MY HEAD.
GO CHANGE YOUR SHIRT. IT LOOKS DIRTY.
© 1995 Washington Post Writers Group
11-16
GEEZ! JUST WHEN YOU THINK YOU'VE GOT A BASIC UNDERSTANDING OF HUMAN ANATOMY THEY THROW SOMETHING LIKE THIS AT YOU.
BRIAN CRANE

PICKLES

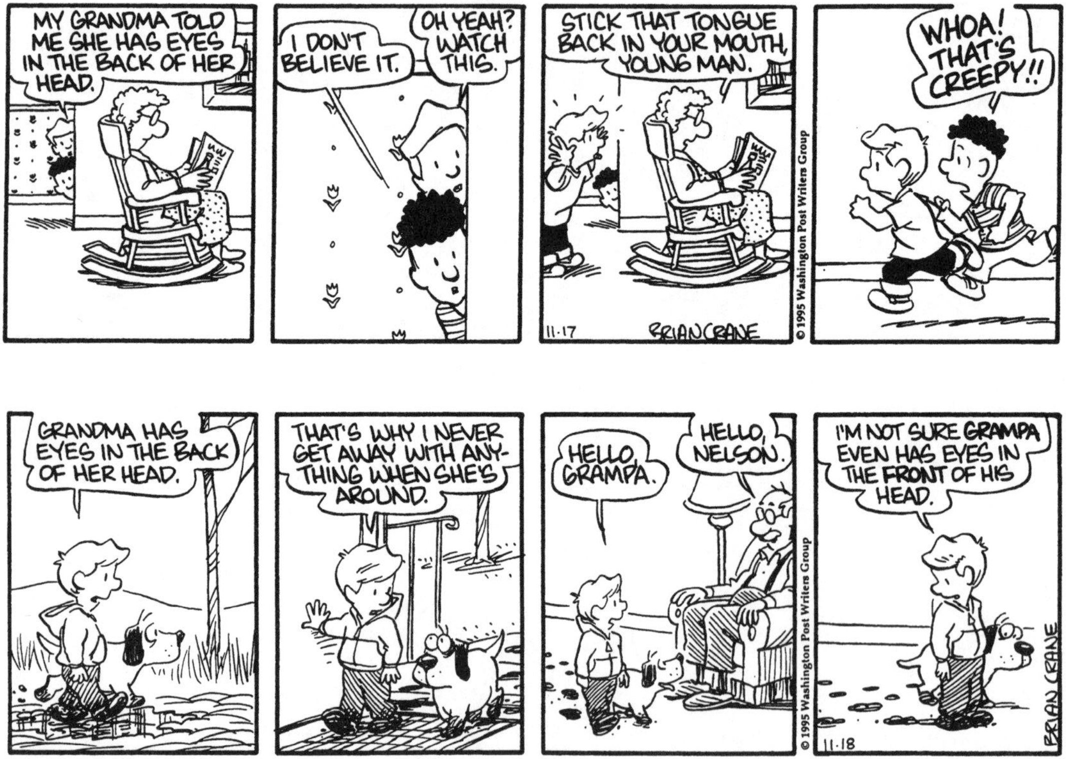
MY GRANDMA TOLD ME SHE HAS EYES IN THE BACK OF HER HEAD.
I DON'T BELIEVE IT.
OH YEAH? WATCH THIS.
STICK THAT TONGUE BACK IN YOUR MOUTH, YOUNG MAN.
11·17
BRIAN CRANE
© 1995 Washington Post Writers Group
WHOA! THAT'S CREEPY!!
GRANDMA HAS EYES IN THE BACK OF HER HEAD.
THAT'S WHY I NEVER GET AWAY WITH ANY-THING WHEN SHE'S AROUND.
HELLO, GRAMPA.
HELLO, NELSON.
© 1995 Washington Post Writers Group
I'M NOT SURE GRAMPA EVEN HAS EYES IN THE FRONT OF HIS HEAD.
11·18
BRIAN CRANE

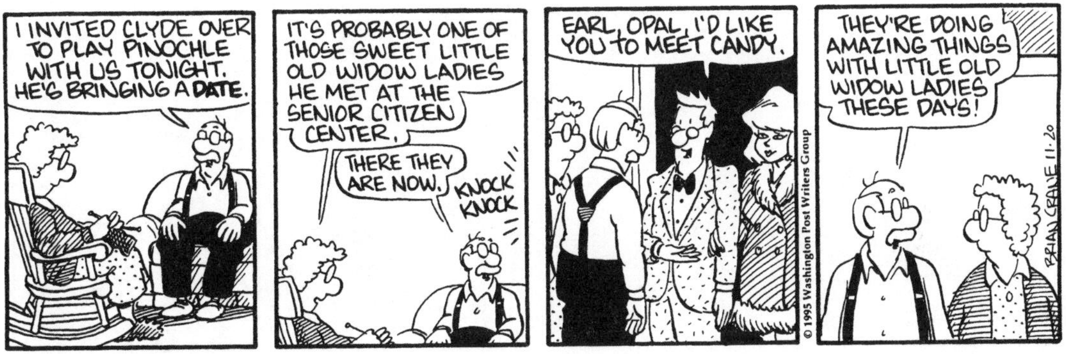
I INVITED CLYDE OVER TO PLAY PINOCHLE WITH US TONIGHT. HE'S BRINGING A **DATE**.
IT'S PROBABLY ONE OF THOSE SWEET LITTLE OLD WIDOW LADIES HE MET AT THE SENIOR CITIZEN CENTER.
THERE THEY ARE NOW.
KNOCK KNOCK
EARL, OPAL, I'D LIKE YOU TO MEET CANDY.
© 1995 Washington Post Writers Group
THEY'RE DOING AMAZING THINGS WITH LITTLE OLD WIDOW LADIES THESE DAYS!
BRIAN CRANE 11-20

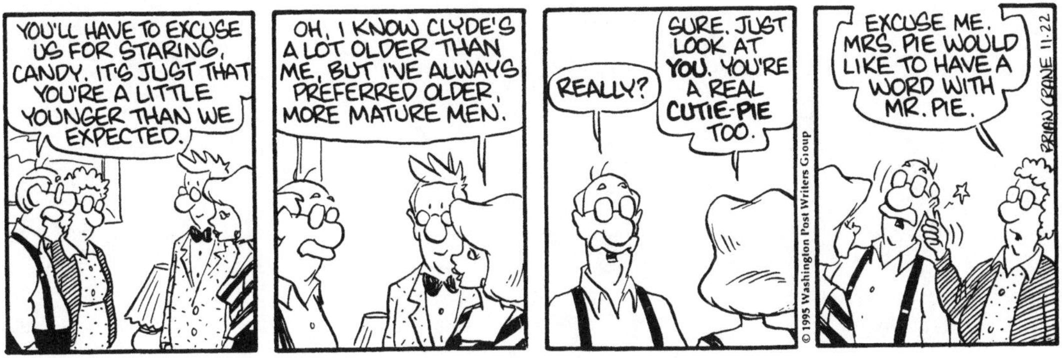
YOU'LL HAVE TO EXCUSE US FOR STARING, CANDY. IT'S JUST THAT YOU'RE A LITTLE YOUNGER THAN WE EXPECTED.
OH, I KNOW CLYDE'S A LOT OLDER THAN ME, BUT I'VE ALWAYS PREFERRED OLDER, MORE MATURE MEN.
REALLY?
SURE. JUST LOOK AT **YOU**. YOU'RE A REAL **CUTIE-PIE** TOO.
© 1995 Washington Post Writers Group
EXCUSE ME. MRS. PIE WOULD LIKE TO HAVE A WORD WITH MR. PIE.
BRIAN CRANE 11-22

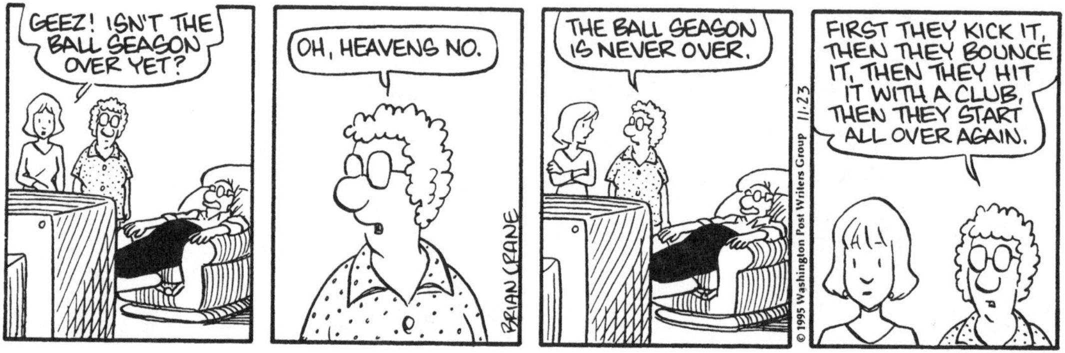
GEEZ! ISN'T THE BALL SEASON OVER YET?
OH, HEAVENS NO.
BRIAN CRANE
THE BALL SEASON IS NEVER OVER.
11.23
© 1995 Washington Post Writers Group
FIRST THEY KICK IT, THEN THEY BOUNCE IT, THEN THEY HIT IT WITH A CLUB, THEN THEY START ALL OVER AGAIN.

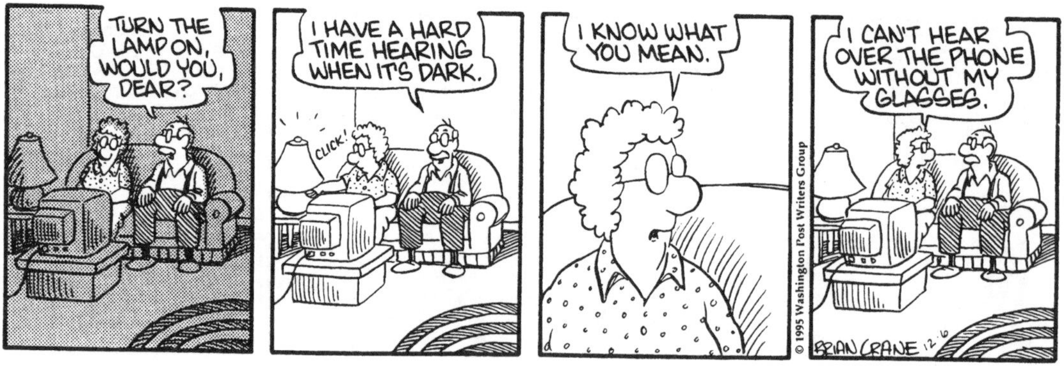
TURN THE LAMP ON, WOULD YOU, DEAR?
I HAVE A HARD TIME HEARING WHEN IT'S DARK.
CLICK!
I KNOW WHAT YOU MEAN.
© 1995 Washington Post Writers Group
I CAN'T HEAR OVER THE PHONE WITHOUT MY GLASSES.
BRIAN CRANE 12.6

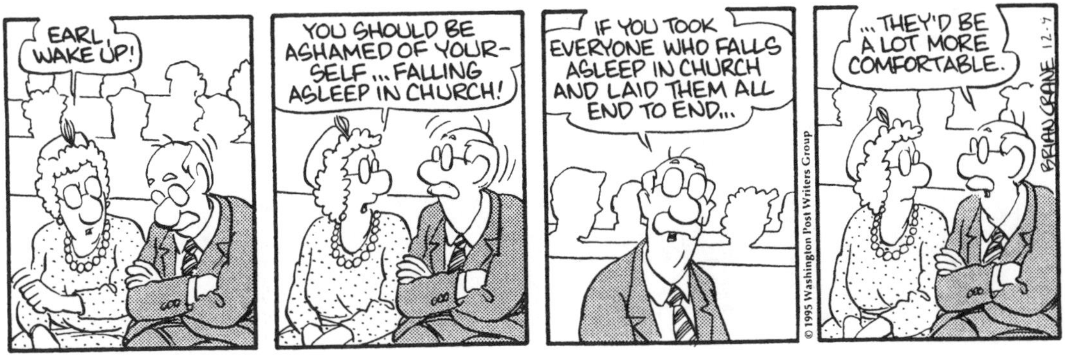
EARL, WAKE UP!
YOU SHOULD BE ASHAMED OF YOURSELF... FALLING ASLEEP IN CHURCH!
IF YOU TOOK EVERYONE WHO FALLS ASLEEP IN CHURCH AND LAID THEM ALL END TO END...
© 1995 Washington Post Writers Group
...THEY'D BE A LOT MORE COMFORTABLE.
12-7
BRIAN CRANE

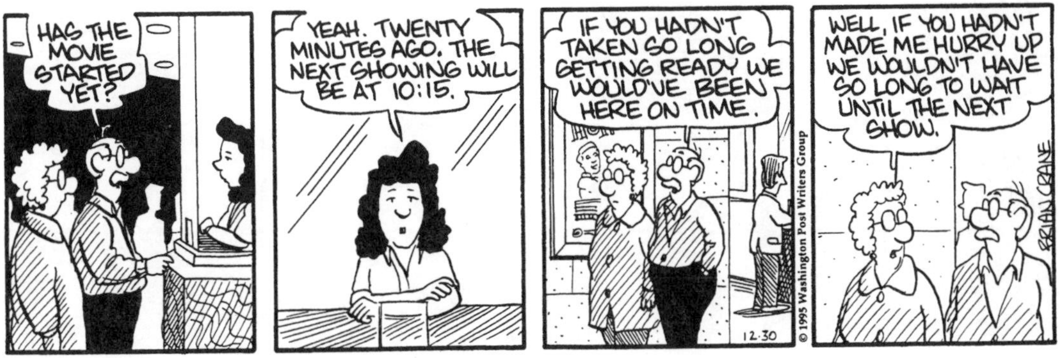
HAS THE MOVIE STARTED YET?
YEAH. TWENTY MINUTES AGO. THE NEXT SHOWING WILL BE AT 10:15.
IF YOU HADN'T TAKEN SO LONG GETTING READY WE WOULD'VE BEEN HERE ON TIME.
12-30
© 1995 Washington Post Writers Group
WELL, IF YOU HADN'T MADE ME HURRY UP WE WOULDN'T HAVE SO LONG TO WAIT UNTIL THE NEXT SHOW.
BRIAN CRANE

PICKLES

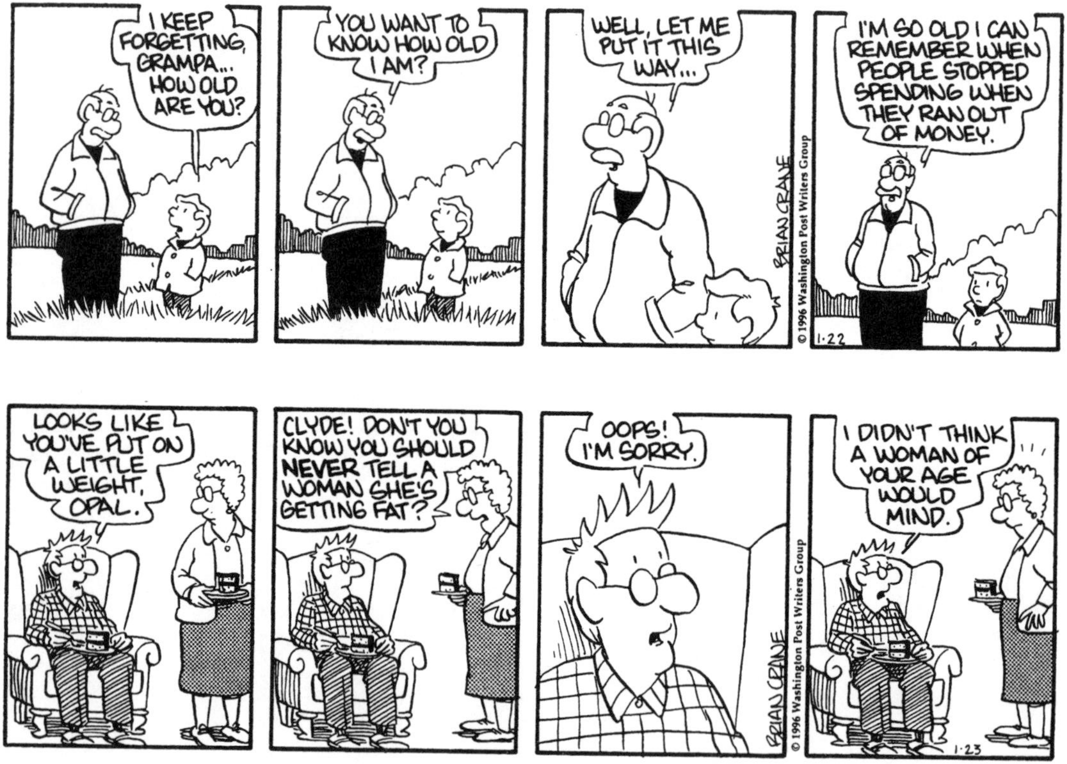
I KEEP FORGETTING, GRAMPA... HOW OLD ARE YOU?
YOU WANT TO KNOW HOW OLD I AM?
WELL, LET ME PUT IT THIS WAY...
I'M SO OLD I CAN REMEMBER WHEN PEOPLE STOPPED SPENDING WHEN THEY RAN OUT OF MONEY.
BRIAN CRANE
© 1996 Washington Post Writers Group
1·22
LOOKS LIKE YOU'VE PUT ON A LITTLE WEIGHT, OPAL.
CLYDE! DON'T YOU KNOW YOU SHOULD NEVER TELL A WOMAN SHE'S GETTING FAT?
OOPS! I'M SORRY.
I DIDN'T THINK A WOMAN OF YOUR AGE WOULD MIND.
BRIAN CRANE
© 1996 Washington Post Writers Group
1·23

PICKLES

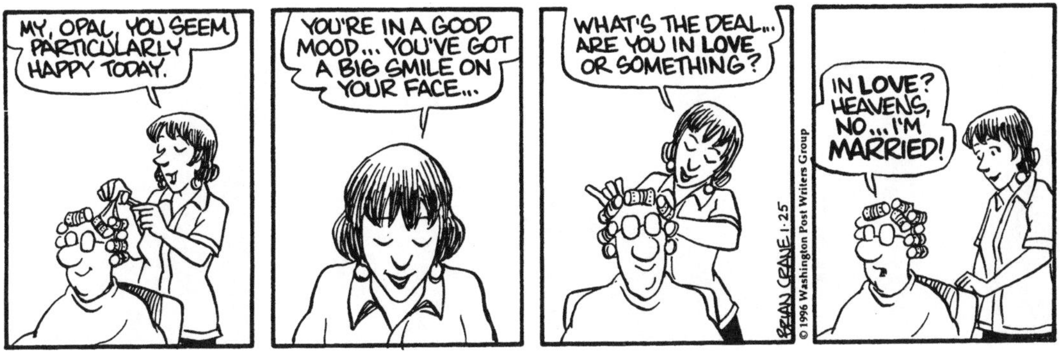
MY, OPAL, YOU SEEM PARTICULARLY HAPPY TODAY.
YOU'RE IN A GOOD MOOD... YOU'VE GOT A BIG SMILE ON YOUR FACE...
WHAT'S THE DEAL... ARE YOU IN LOVE OR SOMETHING?
BRIAN CRANE 1·25
© 1996 Washington Post Writers Group
IN LOVE? HEAVENS, NO... I'M MARRIED!

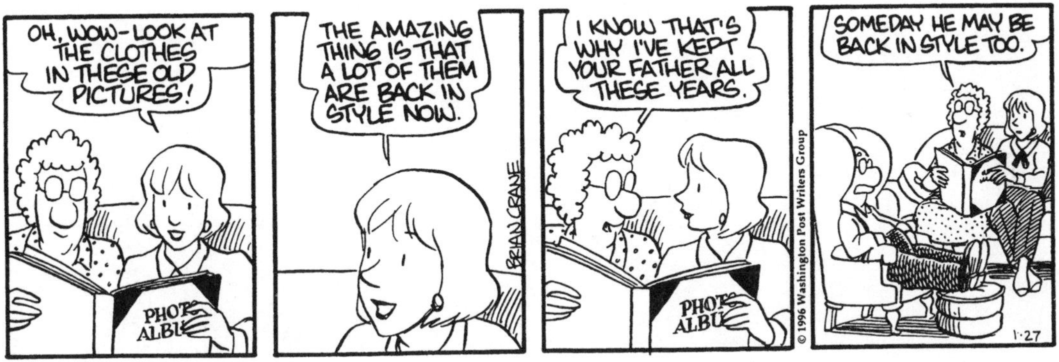
OH, WOW-LOOK AT THE CLOTHES IN THESE OLD PICTURES!
PHOTO ALBUM
THE AMAZING THING IS THAT A LOT OF THEM ARE BACK IN STYLE NOW.
BRIAN CRANE
I KNOW THAT'S WHY I'VE KEPT YOUR FATHER ALL THESE YEARS.
© 1996 Washington Post Writers Group
SOMEDAY HE MAY BE BACK IN STYLE TOO.
1·27

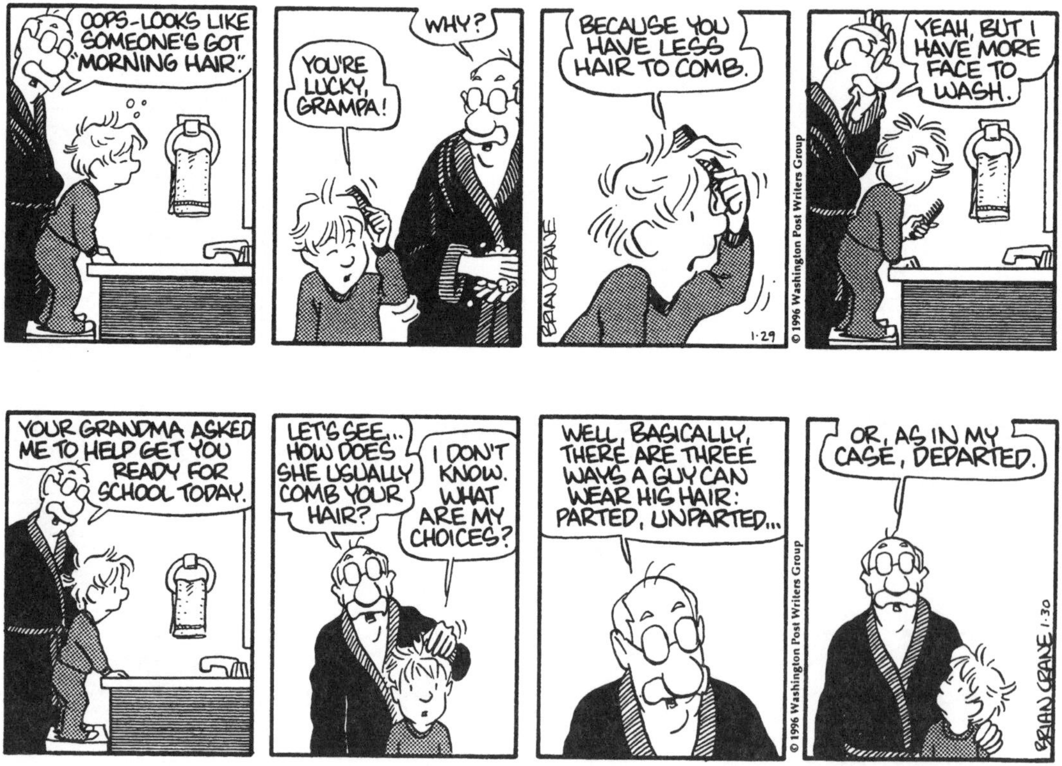
OOPS-LOOKS LIKE SOMEONE'S GOT "MORNING HAIR."
YOU'RE LUCKY, GRAMPA!
WHY?
BECAUSE YOU HAVE LESS HAIR TO COMB.
BRIAN CRANE
1·29
© 1996 Washington Post Writers Group
YEAH, BUT I HAVE MORE FACE TO WASH.
YOUR GRANDMA ASKED ME TO HELP GET YOU READY FOR SCHOOL TODAY.
LET'S SEE... HOW DOES SHE USUALLY COMB YOUR HAIR?
I DON'T KNOW. WHAT ARE MY CHOICES?
WELL, BASICALLY, THERE ARE THREE WAYS A GUY CAN WEAR HIS HAIR: PARTED, UNPARTED...
© 1996 Washington Post Writers Group
OR, AS IN MY CASE, DEPARTED.
BRIAN CRANE 1·30

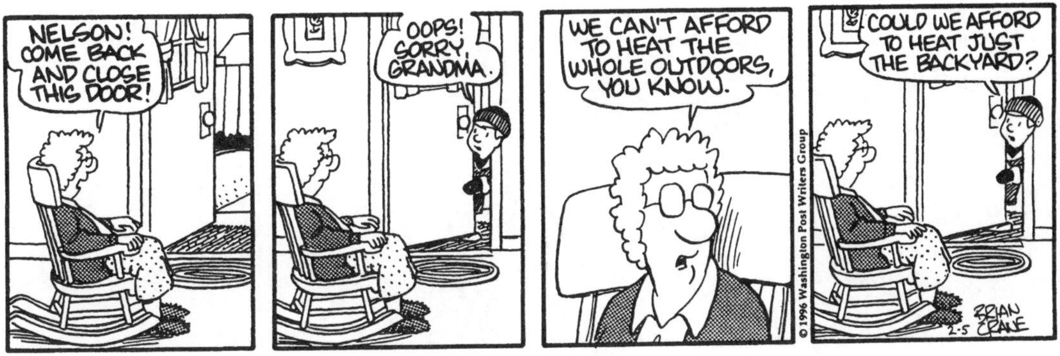
NELSON! COME BACK AND CLOSE THIS DOOR!
OOPS! SORRY, GRANDMA.
WE CAN'T AFFORD TO HEAT THE WHOLE OUTDOORS, YOU KNOW.
COULD WE AFFORD TO HEAT JUST THE BACKYARD?
BRIAN CRANE 2-5
© 1996 Washington Post Writers Group

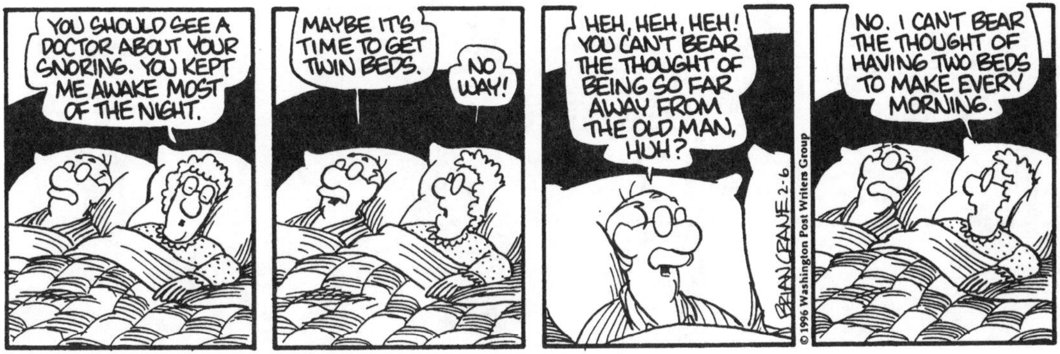
YOU SHOULD SEE A DOCTOR ABOUT YOUR SNORING. YOU KEPT ME AWAKE MOST OF THE NIGHT.
MAYBE IT'S TIME TO GET TWIN BEDS.
NO WAY!
HEH, HEH, HEH! YOU CAN'T BEAR THE THOUGHT OF BEING SO FAR AWAY FROM THE OLD MAN, HUH?
NO. I CAN'T BEAR THE THOUGHT OF HAVING TWO BEDS TO MAKE EVERY MORNING.
BRIAN CRANE 2-6
© 1996 Washington Post Writers Group

PICKLES

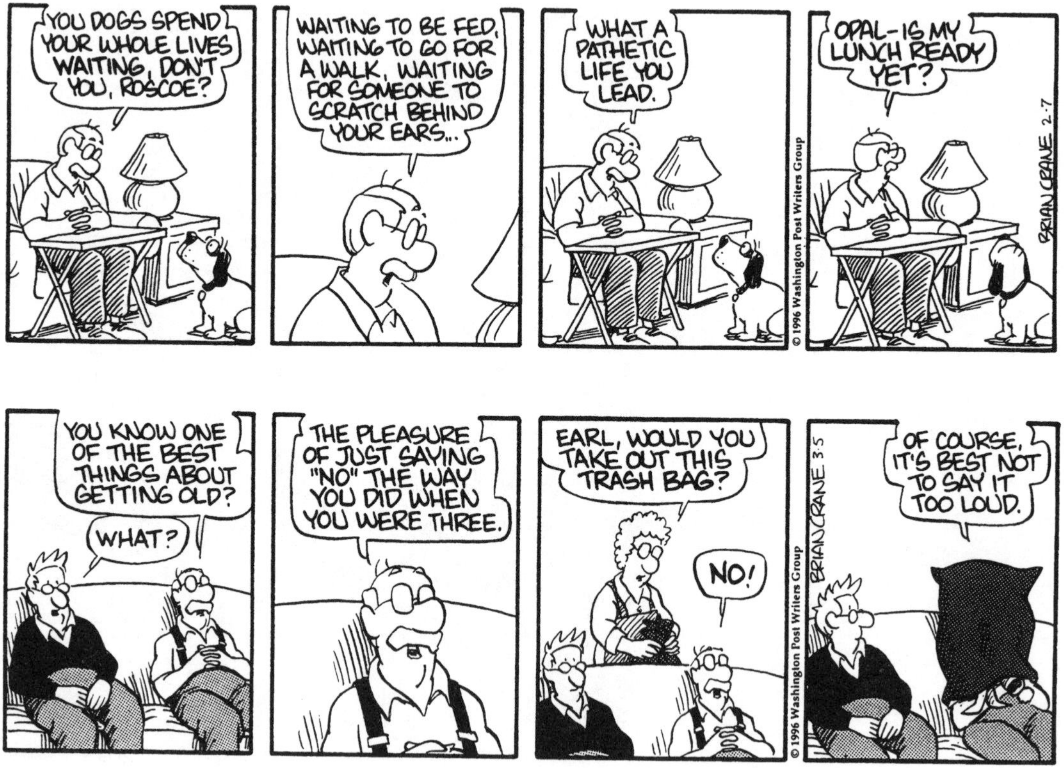
YOU DOGS SPEND YOUR WHOLE LIVES WAITING, DON'T YOU, ROSCOE?
WAITING TO BE FED, WAITING TO GO FOR A WALK, WAITING FOR SOMEONE TO SCRATCH BEHIND YOUR EARS...
WHAT A PATHETIC LIFE YOU LEAD.
OPAL-IS MY LUNCH READY YET?
© 1996 Washington Post Writers Group
BRIAN CRANE 2-7
YOU KNOW ONE OF THE BEST THINGS ABOUT GETTING OLD?
WHAT?
THE PLEASURE OF JUST SAYING "NO" THE WAY YOU DID WHEN YOU WERE THREE.
EARL, WOULD YOU TAKE OUT THIS TRASH BAG?
NO!
© 1996 Washington Post Writers Group
BRIAN CRANE 3-5
OF COURSE, IT'S BEST NOT TO SAY IT TOO LOUD.

PICKLES

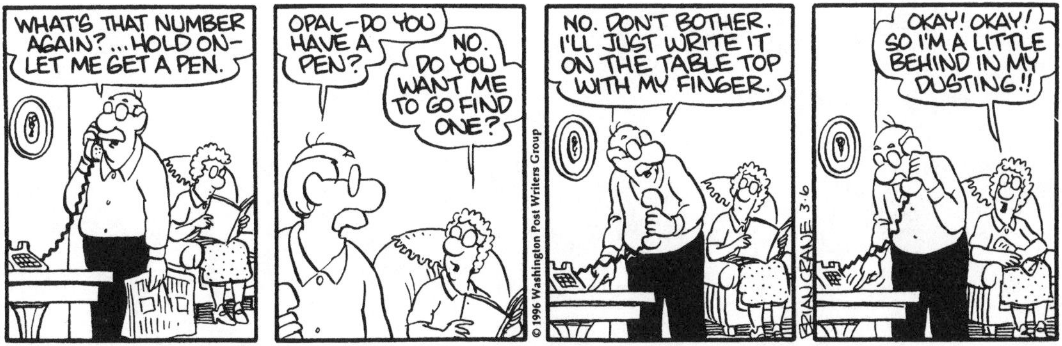
WHAT'S THAT NUMBER AGAIN? ...HOLD ON- LET ME GET A PEN.
OPAL-DO YOU HAVE A PEN?
NO. DO YOU WANT ME TO GO FIND ONE?
© 1996 Washington Post Writers Group
NO. DON'T BOTHER. I'LL JUST WRITE IT ON THE TABLE TOP WITH MY FINGER.
BRIAN CRANE 3·6
OKAY! OKAY! SO I'M A LITTLE BEHIND IN MY DUSTING!!

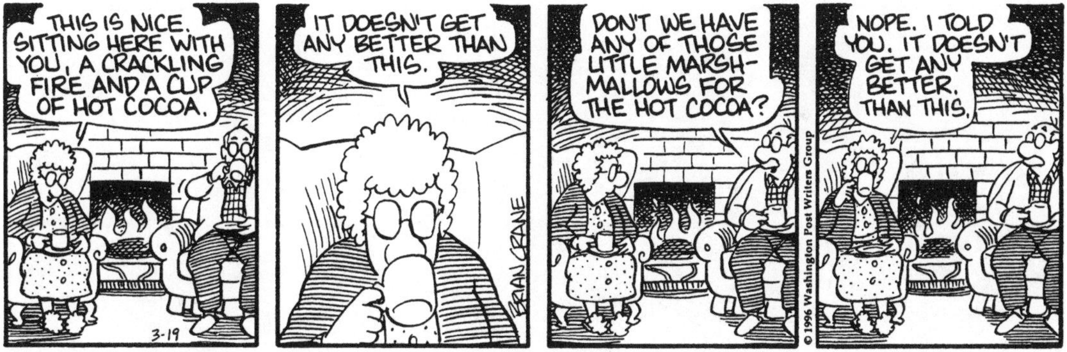
THIS IS NICE. SITTING HERE WITH YOU, A CRACKLING FIRE AND A CUP OF HOT COCOA.
3-19
IT DOESN'T GET ANY BETTER THAN THIS.
BRIAN CRANE
DON'T WE HAVE ANY OF THOSE LITTLE MARSH-MALLOWS FOR THE HOT COCOA?
© 1996 Washington Post Writers Group
NOPE. I TOLD YOU. IT DOESN'T GET ANY BETTER THAN THIS.

PICKLES

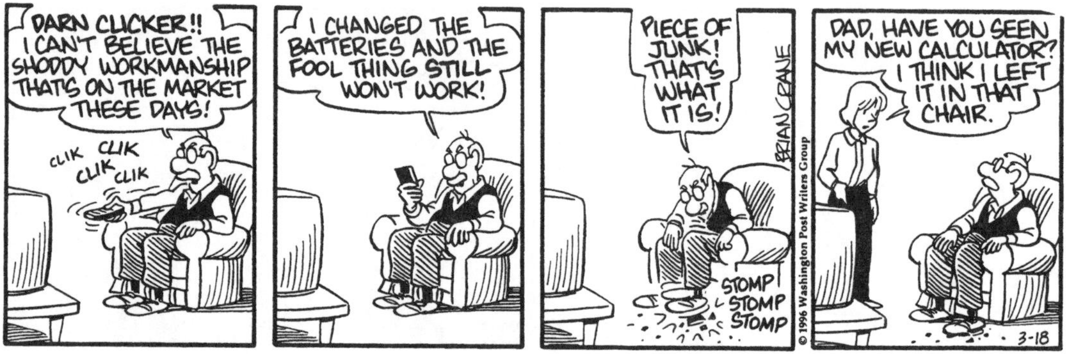

DARN CLICKER!! I CAN'T BELIEVE THE SHODDY WORKMANSHIP THAT'S ON THE MARKET THESE DAYS!
CLIK CLIK CLIK CLIK
I CHANGED THE BATTERIES AND THE FOOL THING STILL WON'T WORK!
PIECE OF JUNK! THAT'S WHAT IT IS!
STOMP STOMP STOMP
BRIAN CRANE
© 1996 Washington Post Writers Group
DAD, HAVE YOU SEEN MY NEW CALCULATOR? I THINK I LEFT IT IN THAT CHAIR.
3-18

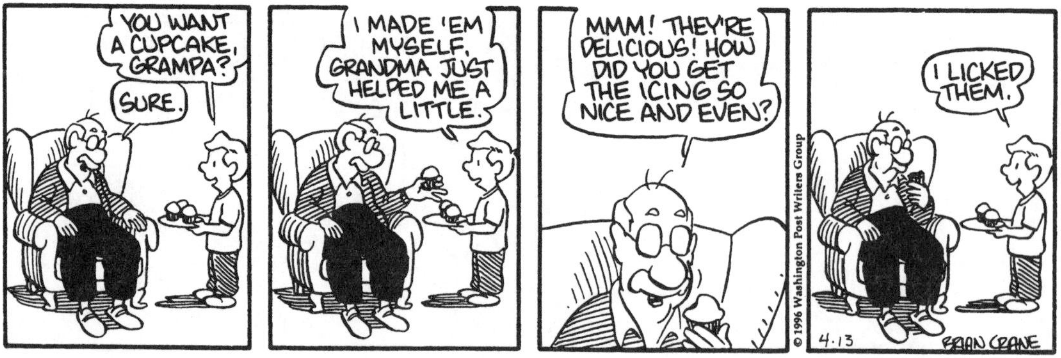

YOU WANT A CUPCAKE, GRAMPA?
SURE.
I MADE 'EM MYSELF. GRANDMA JUST HELPED ME A LITTLE.
MMM! THEY'RE DELICIOUS! HOW DID YOU GET THE ICING SO NICE AND EVEN?
© 1996 Washington Post Writers Group
I LICKED THEM.
4-13
BRIAN CRANE

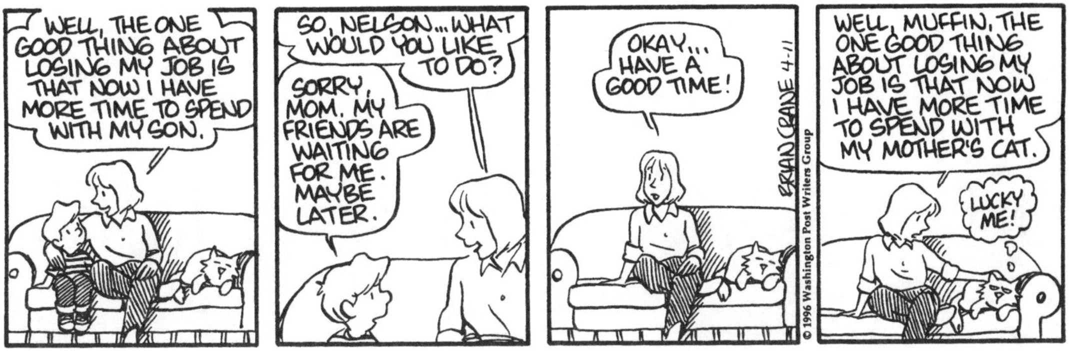
WELL, THE ONE GOOD THING ABOUT LOSING MY JOB IS THAT NOW I HAVE MORE TIME TO SPEND WITH MY SON.
SO, NELSON... WHAT WOULD YOU LIKE TO DO?
SORRY, MOM. MY FRIENDS ARE WAITING FOR ME. MAYBE LATER.
OKAY,... HAVE A GOOD TIME!
4-11
BRIAN CRANE
© 1996 Washington Post Writers Group
WELL, MUFFIN, THE ONE GOOD THING ABOUT LOSING MY JOB IS THAT NOW I HAVE MORE TIME TO SPEND WITH MY MOTHER'S CAT.
LUCKY ME!

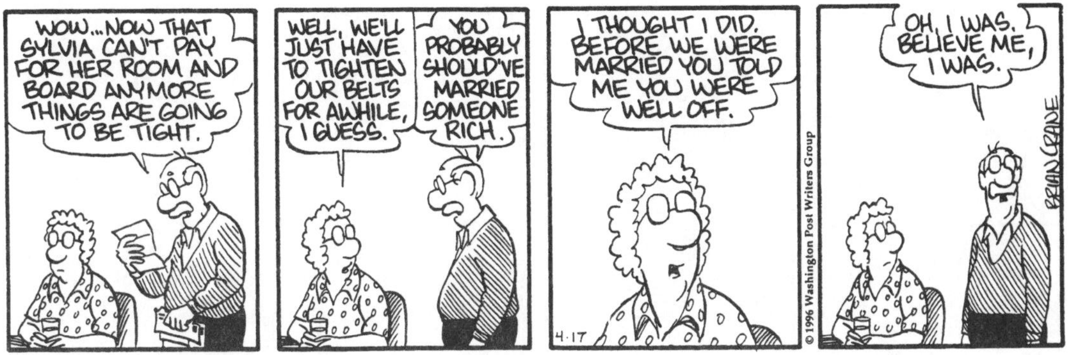
WOW... NOW THAT SYLVIA CAN'T PAY FOR HER ROOM AND BOARD ANYMORE THINGS ARE GOING TO BE TIGHT.
WELL, WE'LL JUST HAVE TO TIGHTEN OUR BELTS FOR AWHILE, I GUESS.
YOU PROBABLY SHOULD'VE MARRIED SOMEONE RICH.
I THOUGHT I DID. BEFORE WE WERE MARRIED YOU TOLD ME YOU WERE WELL OFF.
4-17
© 1996 Washington Post Writers Group
OH, I WAS. BELIEVE ME, I WAS.
BRIAN CRANE

PICKLES

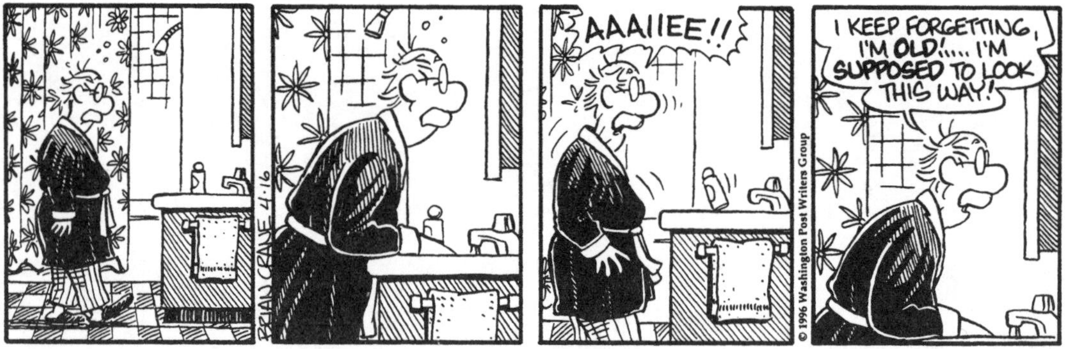
AAAIIEE!!
I KEEP FORGETTING, I'M OLD!.... I'M SUPPOSED TO LOOK THIS WAY!
BRIAN CRANE 4·16
© 1996 Washington Post Writers Group

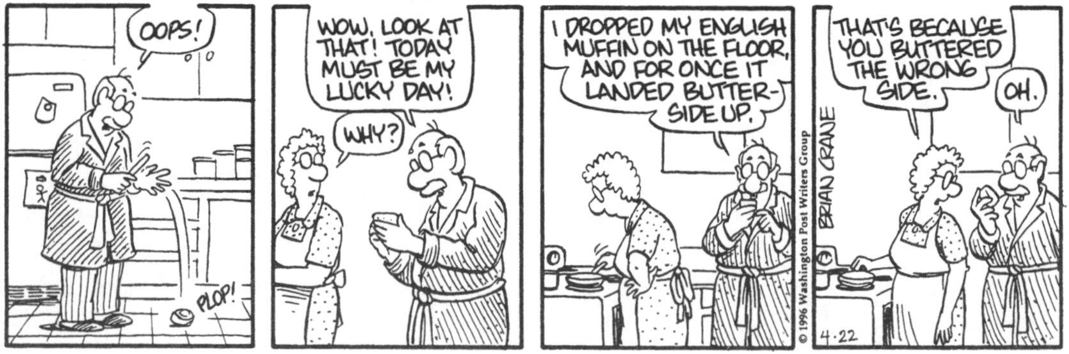
OOPS!
PLOP!
WOW, LOOK AT THAT! TODAY MUST BE MY LUCKY DAY!
WHY?
I DROPPED MY ENGLISH MUFFIN ON THE FLOOR, AND FOR ONCE IT LANDED BUTTER-SIDE UP.
THAT'S BECAUSE YOU BUTTERED THE WRONG SIDE.
OH.
© 1996 Washington Post Writers Group
BRIAN CRANE
4·22

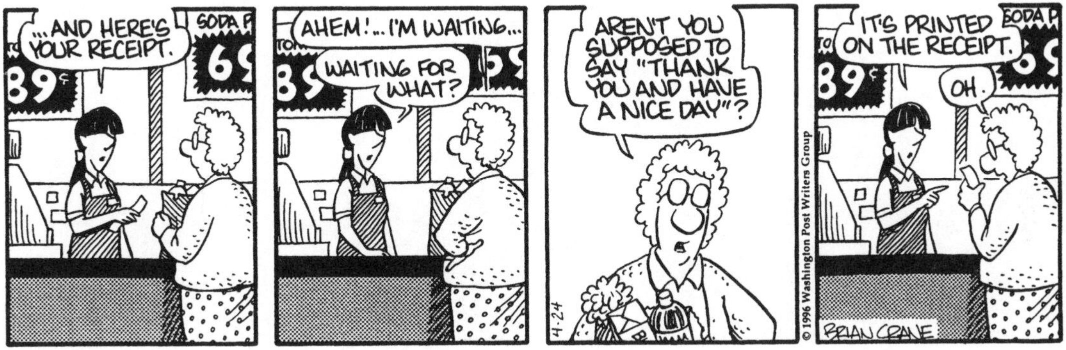
...AND HERE'S YOUR RECEIPT.
SODA P
89¢
69
AHEM! ... I'M WAITING...
WAITING FOR WHAT?
AREN'T YOU SUPPOSED TO SAY "THANK YOU AND HAVE A NICE DAY"?
4-24
© 1996 Washington Post Writers Group
IT'S PRINTED ON THE RECEIPT.
OH.
BRIAN CRANE

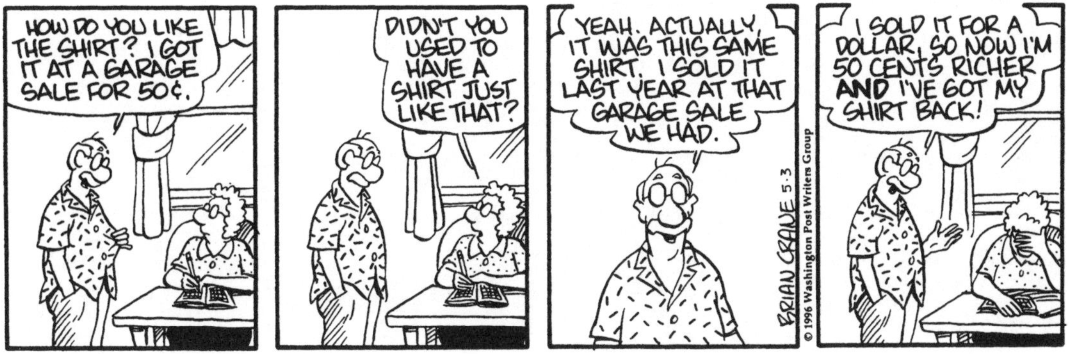
HOW DO YOU LIKE THE SHIRT? I GOT IT AT A GARAGE SALE FOR 50¢.
DIDN'T YOU USED TO HAVE A SHIRT JUST LIKE THAT?
YEAH. ACTUALLY, IT WAS THIS SAME SHIRT. I SOLD IT LAST YEAR AT THAT GARAGE SALE WE HAD.
BRIAN CRANE 5-3
© 1996 Washington Post Writers Group
I SOLD IT FOR A DOLLAR, SO NOW I'M 50 CENTS RICHER **AND** I'VE GOT MY SHIRT BACK!

PICKLES

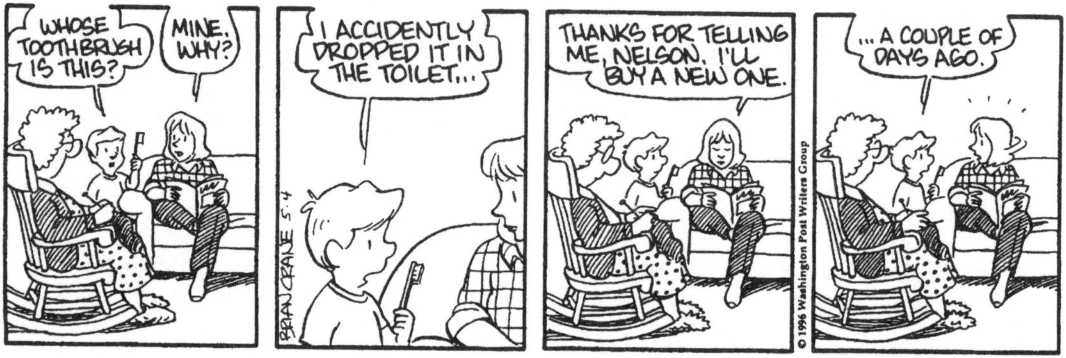
WHOSE TOOTHBRUSH IS THIS?
MINE. WHY?
I ACCIDENTLY DROPPED IT IN THE TOILET...
BRIAN CRANE 5-4
THANKS FOR TELLING ME, NELSON. I'LL BUY A NEW ONE.
© 1996 Washington Post Writers Group
...A COUPLE OF DAYS AGO.

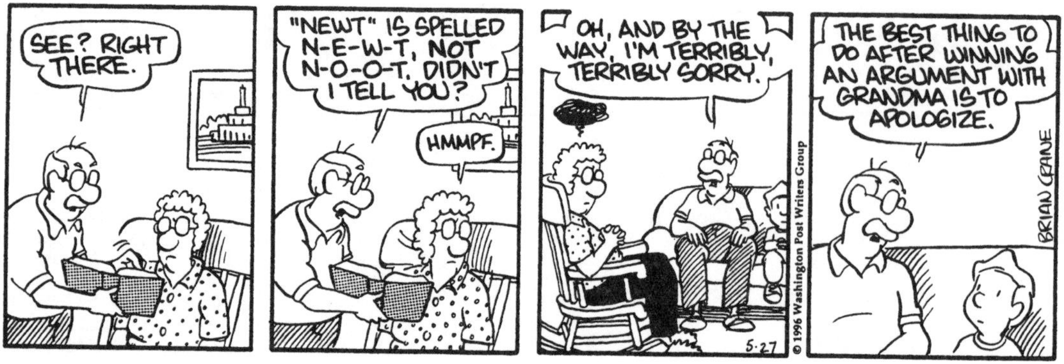
SEE? RIGHT THERE.
"NEWT" IS SPELLED N-E-W-T, NOT N-O-O-T. DIDN'T I TELL YOU?
HMMPF.
OH, AND BY THE WAY, I'M TERRIBLY, TERRIBLY SORRY.
5-27
© 1996 Washington Post Writers Group
THE BEST THING TO DO AFTER WINNING AN ARGUMENT WITH GRANDMA IS TO APOLOGIZE.
BRIAN CRANE

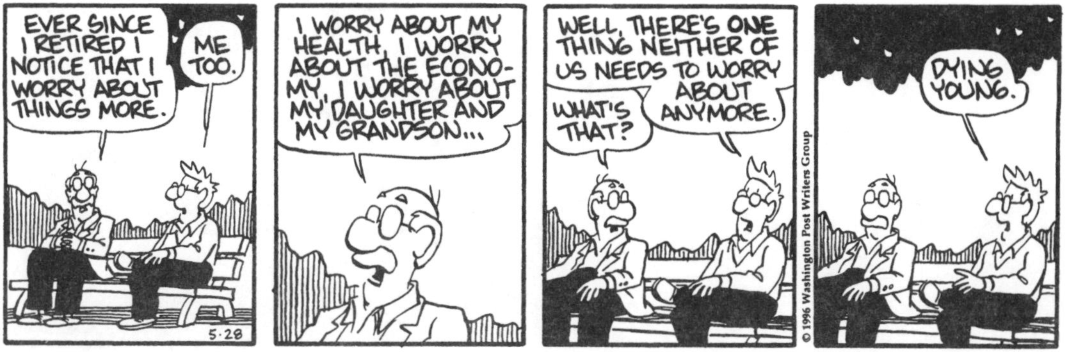
EVER SINCE I RETIRED I NOTICE THAT I WORRY ABOUT THINGS MORE.
ME TOO.
5·28
I WORRY ABOUT MY HEALTH, I WORRY ABOUT THE ECONOMY, I WORRY ABOUT MY DAUGHTER AND MY GRANDSON...
WELL, THERE'S ONE THING NEITHER OF US NEEDS TO WORRY ABOUT ANYMORE.
WHAT'S THAT?
© 1996 Washington Post Writers Group
DYING YOUNG.

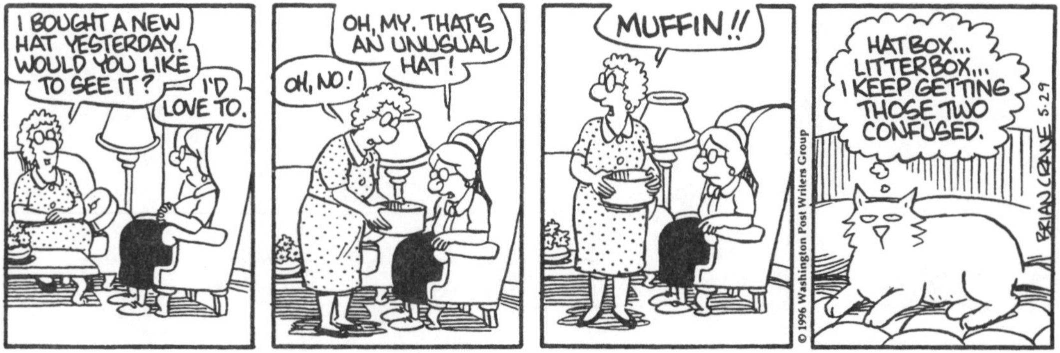
I BOUGHT A NEW HAT YESTERDAY. WOULD YOU LIKE TO SEE IT?
I'D LOVE TO.
OH, MY. THAT'S AN UNUSUAL HAT!
OH, NO!
MUFFIN!!
© 1996 Washington Post Writers Group
HATBOX... LITTERBOX... I KEEP GETTING THOSE TWO CONFUSED.
5·29
BRIAN CRANE

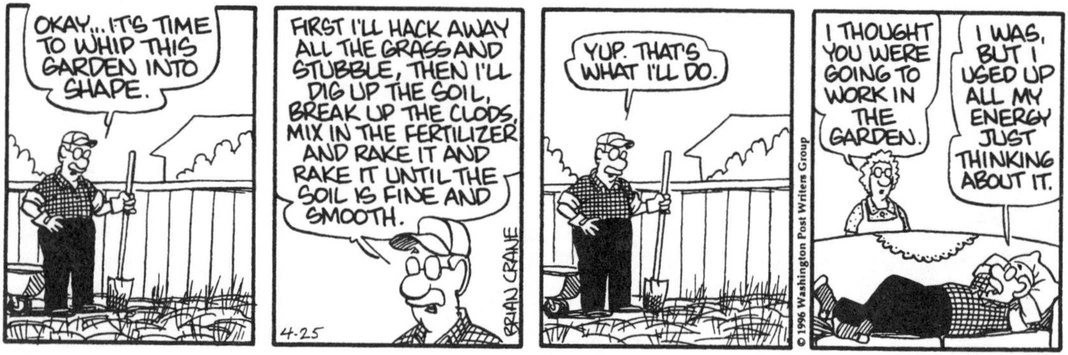
OKAY... IT'S TIME TO WHIP THIS GARDEN INTO SHAPE.
FIRST I'LL HACK AWAY ALL THE GRASS AND STUBBLE, THEN I'LL DIG UP THE SOIL, BREAK UP THE CLODS, MIX IN THE FERTILIZER AND RAKE IT AND RAKE IT UNTIL THE SOIL IS FINE AND SMOOTH.
4-25
BRIAN CRANE
YUP. THAT'S WHAT I'LL DO.
© 1996 Washington Post Writers Group
I THOUGHT YOU WERE GOING TO WORK IN THE GARDEN.
I WAS, BUT I USED UP ALL MY ENERGY JUST THINKING ABOUT IT.

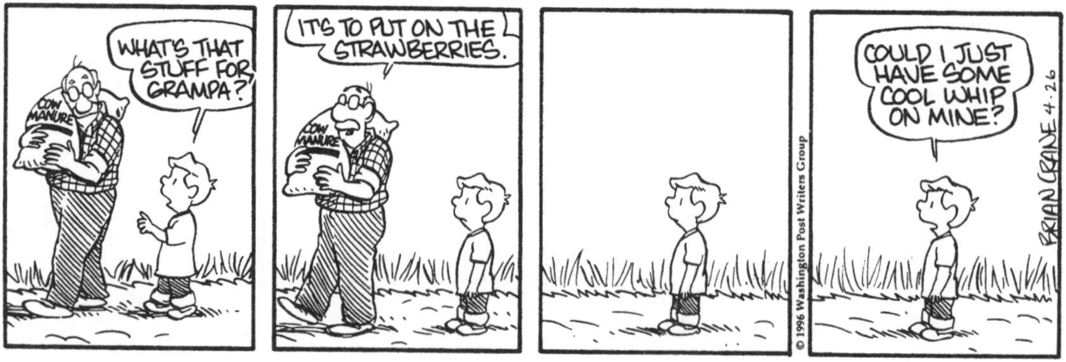
COW MANURE
WHAT'S THAT STUFF FOR GRAMPA?
IT'S TO PUT ON THE STRAWBERRIES.
COW MANURE
© 1996 Washington Post Writers Group
COULD I JUST HAVE SOME COOL WHIP ON MINE?
BRIAN CRANE 4-26

PICKLES

IT'S HARD TO BELIEVE YOU AND OPAL WILL SOON BE CELEBRATING YOUR FIFTIETH WEDDING ANNIVERSARY.

YEAH, I KNOW.

WHAT'S YOUR SECRET FOR STAYING MARRIED SUCH A LONG TIME?

SIMPLE.

ONE OF US TALKS AND THE OTHER ONE DOESN'T LISTEN.

BRIAN CRANE 5-30

© 1996 Washington Post Writers Group

HMM...

WHAT?

OH, I WAS JUST THINKING...

LIFE IS FULL OF CONTRADICTIONS.

5-31

© 1996 Washington Post Writers Group

IT IS NOT.

43

PICKLES

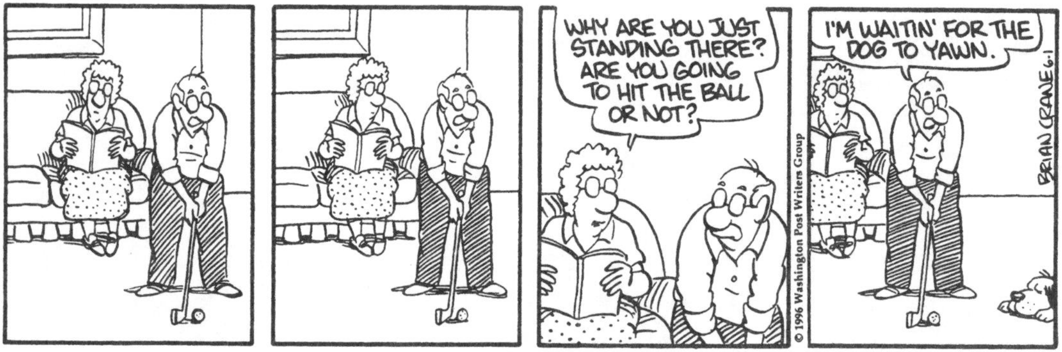
WHY ARE YOU JUST STANDING THERE? ARE YOU GOING TO HIT THE BALL OR NOT?
© 1996 Washington Post Writers Group
I'M WAITIN' FOR THE DOG TO YAWN.
BRIAN CRANE 6-1

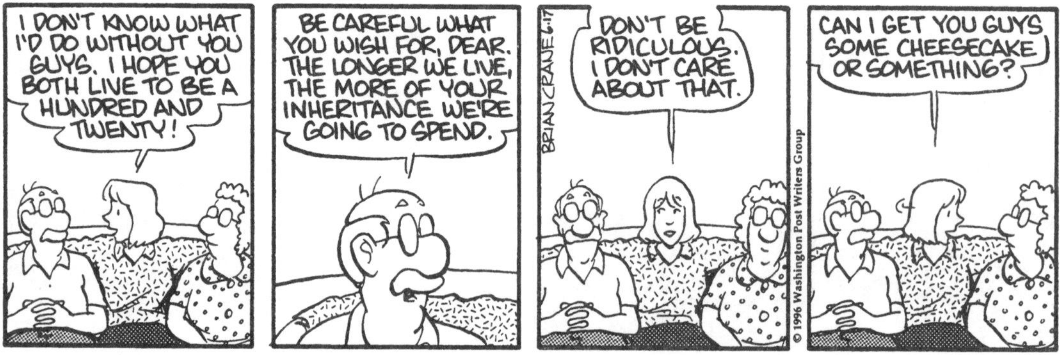
I DON'T KNOW WHAT I'D DO WITHOUT YOU GUYS. I HOPE YOU BOTH LIVE TO BE A HUNDRED AND TWENTY!
BE CAREFUL WHAT YOU WISH FOR, DEAR. THE LONGER WE LIVE, THE MORE OF YOUR INHERITANCE WE'RE GOING TO SPEND.
BRIAN CRANE 6-17
DON'T BE RIDICULOUS. I DON'T CARE ABOUT THAT.
© 1996 Washington Post Writers Group
CAN I GET YOU GUYS SOME CHEESECAKE OR SOMETHING?

PICKLES

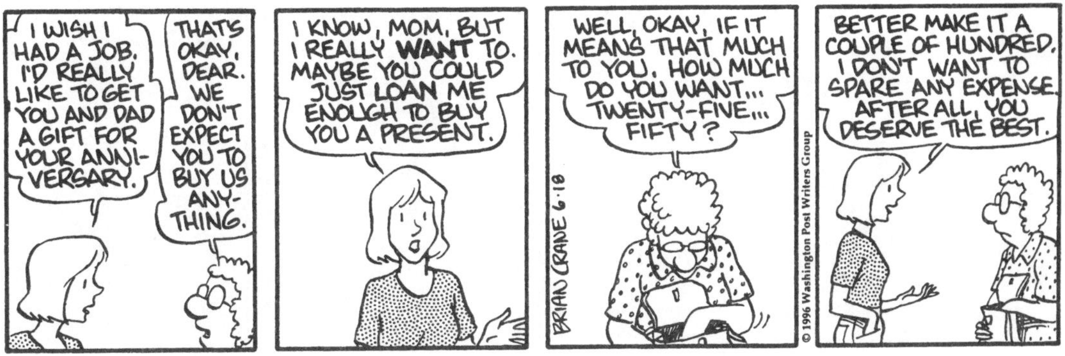

I WISH I HAD A JOB. I'D REALLY LIKE TO GET YOU AND DAD A GIFT FOR YOUR ANNI-VERSARY.
THAT'S OKAY, DEAR. WE DON'T EXPECT YOU TO BUY US ANY-THING.
I KNOW, MOM, BUT I REALLY **WANT** TO. MAYBE YOU COULD JUST LOAN ME ENOUGH TO BUY YOU A PRESENT.
WELL, OKAY, IF IT MEANS THAT MUCH TO YOU. HOW MUCH DO YOU WANT... TWENTY-FIVE... FIFTY?
BRIAN CRANE 6·18
BETTER MAKE IT A COUPLE OF HUNDRED. I DON'T WANT TO SPARE ANY EXPENSE. AFTER ALL, YOU DESERVE THE BEST.
© 1996 Washington Post Writers Group

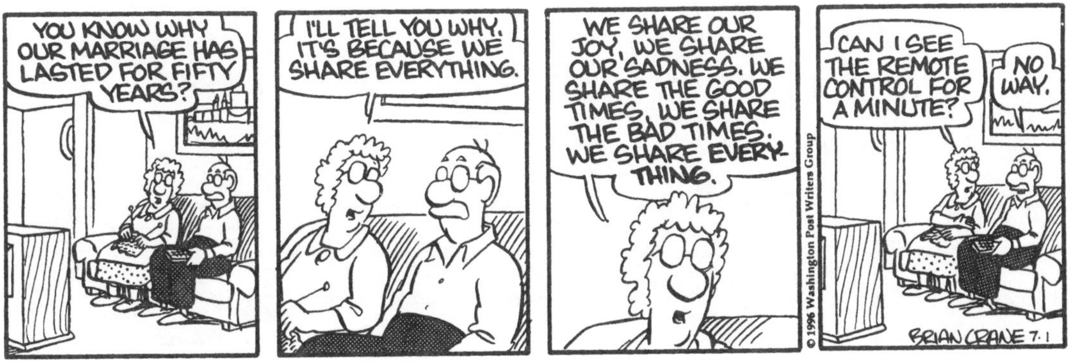

YOU KNOW WHY OUR MARRIAGE HAS LASTED FOR FIFTY YEARS?
I'LL TELL YOU WHY. IT'S BECAUSE WE SHARE EVERYTHING.
WE SHARE OUR JOY, WE SHARE OUR SADNESS. WE SHARE THE GOOD TIMES, WE SHARE THE BAD TIMES. WE SHARE **EVERY-THING**.
© 1996 Washington Post Writers Group
CAN I SEE THE REMOTE CONTROL FOR A MINUTE?
NO WAY.
BRIAN CRANE 7·1

PICKLES

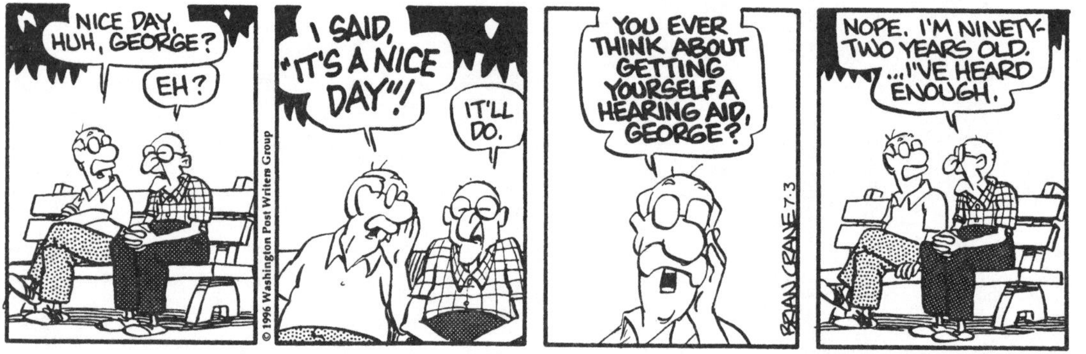
NICE DAY, HUH, GEORGE?
EH?
I SAID, "IT'S A NICE DAY"!
IT'LL DO.
YOU EVER THINK ABOUT GETTING YOURSELF A HEARING AID, GEORGE?
NOPE. I'M NINETY-TWO YEARS OLD. ...I'VE HEARD ENOUGH.
© 1996 Washington Post Writers Group
BRIAN CRANE 7-3

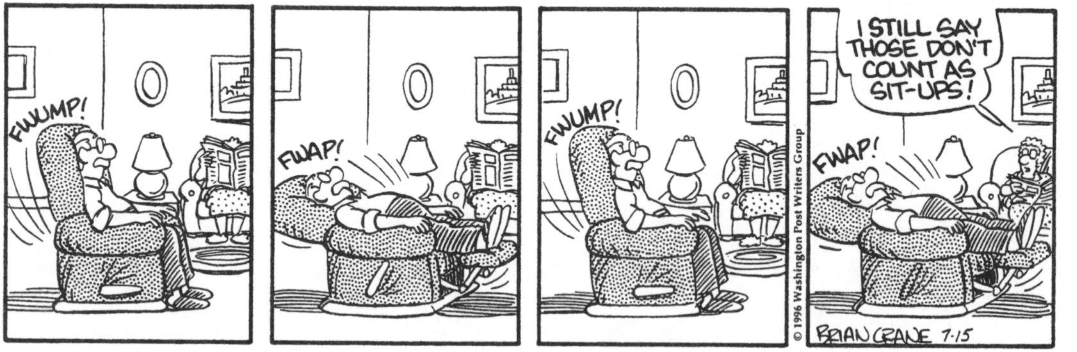
FWUMP!
FWAP!
FWUMP!
I STILL SAY THOSE DON'T COUNT AS SIT-UPS!
FWAP!
© 1996 Washington Post Writers Group
BRIAN CRANE 7-15

PICKLES

HERE YOU GO, NELSON. I'D LIKE TO REDEEM THIS.
IT'S THE COUPON YOU GAVE ME FOR MOTHER'S DAY. REMEMBER?
IT SAYS THAT YOU'LL DO THE DISHES FOR ME FOR ONE WHOLE WEEK.
YEAH, BUT IF YOU'LL NOTICE THE SMALL PRINT, THIS EXPIRED JUNE 30TH.
© 1996 Washington Post Writers Group
BRIAN CRANE 7.17

YOU'LL BE DRIVING A CAR SOMEDAY, NELSON.
YOU'RE GOING TO HAVE TO LEARN TO WATCH OUT FOR ALL THE IDIOTS ON THE ROAD.
JUST REMEMBER...
...THE ONES GOING SLOWER THAN YOU ARE NINCOMPOOPS AND THE ONES GOING FASTER THAN YOU ARE LUNATICS.
© 1996 Washington Post Writers Group
BRIAN CRANE 7.18

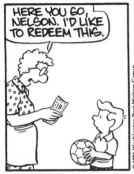

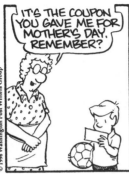

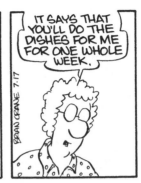

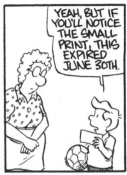

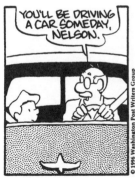

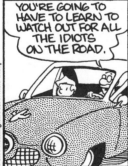

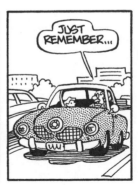

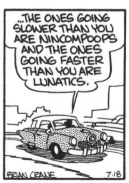

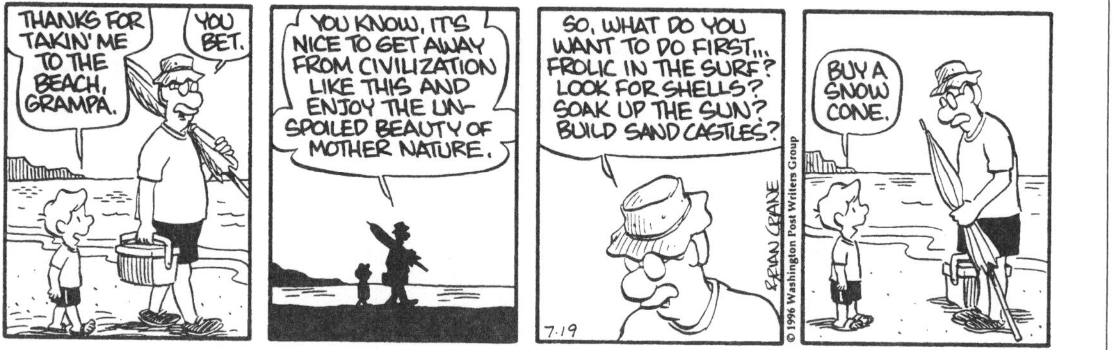
THANKS FOR TAKIN' ME TO THE BEACH, GRAMPA.
YOU BET.
YOU KNOW, IT'S NICE TO GET AWAY FROM CIVILIZATION LIKE THIS AND ENJOY THE UN-SPOILED BEAUTY OF MOTHER NATURE.
SO, WHAT DO YOU WANT TO DO FIRST... FROLIC IN THE SURF? LOOK FOR SHELLS? SOAK UP THE SUN? BUILD SAND CASTLES?
7.19
BRIAN CRANE
© 1996 Washington Post Writers Group
BUY A SNOW CONE.

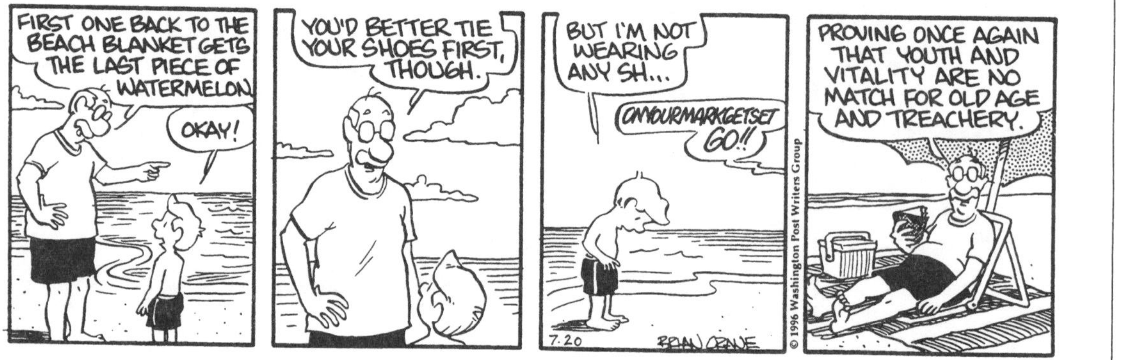
FIRST ONE BACK TO THE BEACH BLANKET GETS THE LAST PIECE OF WATERMELON.
OKAY!
YOU'D BETTER TIE YOUR SHOES FIRST, THOUGH.
BUT I'M NOT WEARING ANY SH...
ONYOURMARKGETSET GO!!
7.20
BRIAN CRANE
© 1996 Washington Post Writers Group
PROVING ONCE AGAIN THAT YOUTH AND VITALITY ARE NO MATCH FOR OLD AGE AND TREACHERY.

YOU EVER KEEP ANY SECRETS FROM YOUR WIFE?
NOPE.
7-25
NEVER. NOT EVEN ONCE.
© 1996 Washington Post Writers Group
BRIAN CRANE
MIND YOU, I **TRIED** LOTS OF TIMES, THOUGH.

LOOK AT THAT CLOUD. IT LOOKS JUST LIKE A PILE OF MASHED POTATOES, DOESN'T IT?
YEAH.
© 1996 Washington Post Writers Group
THAT ONE OVER THERE LOOKS LIKE MASHED POTATOES TOO.
AND SO DOES THAT ONE OVER THERE.
YOU DON'T HAVE A LOT OF IMAGINATION, DO YOU, GRAMPA?
7-27
BRIAN CRANE

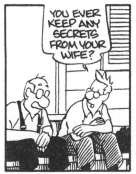

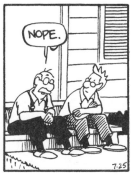

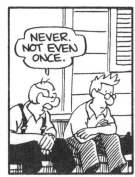

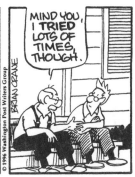

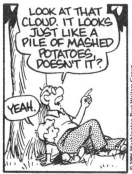

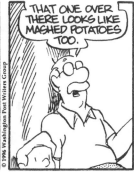

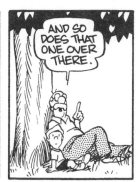

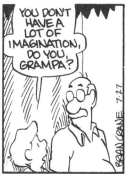

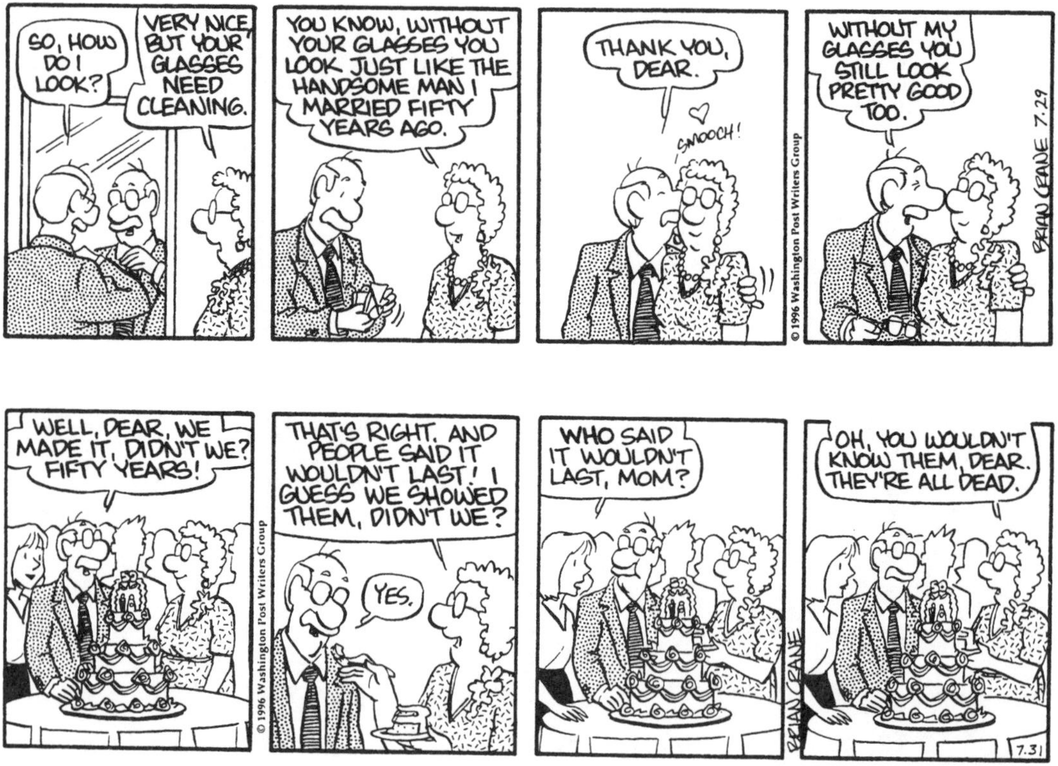
SO, HOW DO I LOOK?
VERY NICE, BUT YOUR GLASSES NEED CLEANING.
YOU KNOW, WITHOUT YOUR GLASSES YOU LOOK JUST LIKE THE HANDSOME MAN I MARRIED FIFTY YEARS AGO.
THANK YOU, DEAR.
SMOOCH!
WITHOUT MY GLASSES YOU STILL LOOK PRETTY GOOD TOO.
BRIAN CRANE 7.29
© 1996 Washington Post Writers Group
WELL, DEAR, WE MADE IT, DIDN'T WE? FIFTY YEARS!
© 1996 Washington Post Writers Group
THAT'S RIGHT. AND PEOPLE SAID IT WOULDN'T LAST! I GUESS WE SHOWED THEM, DIDN'T WE?
YES.
WHO SAID IT WOULDN'T LAST, MOM?
BRIAN CRANE
OH, YOU WOULDN'T KNOW THEM, DEAR. THEY'RE ALL DEAD.
7.31

PICKLES

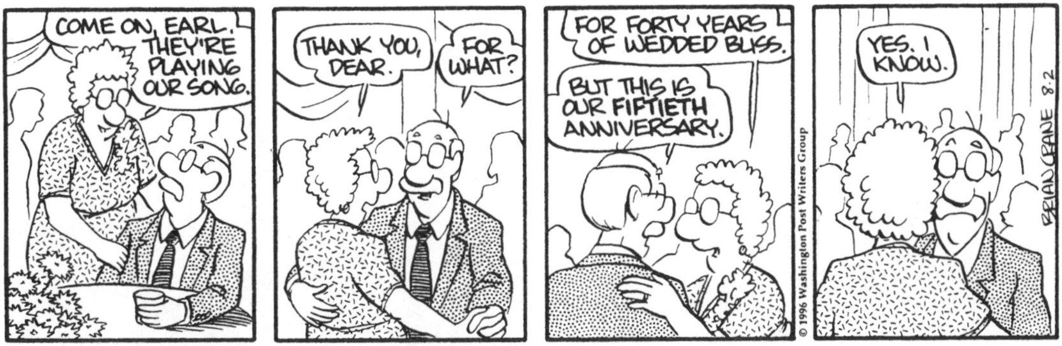

COME ON, EARL. THEY'RE PLAYING OUR SONG.
THANK YOU, DEAR.
FOR WHAT?
FOR FORTY YEARS OF WEDDED BLISS.
BUT THIS IS OUR FIFTIETH ANNIVERSARY.
YES. I KNOW.
BRIAN CRANE 8·2
© 1996 Washington Post Writers Group

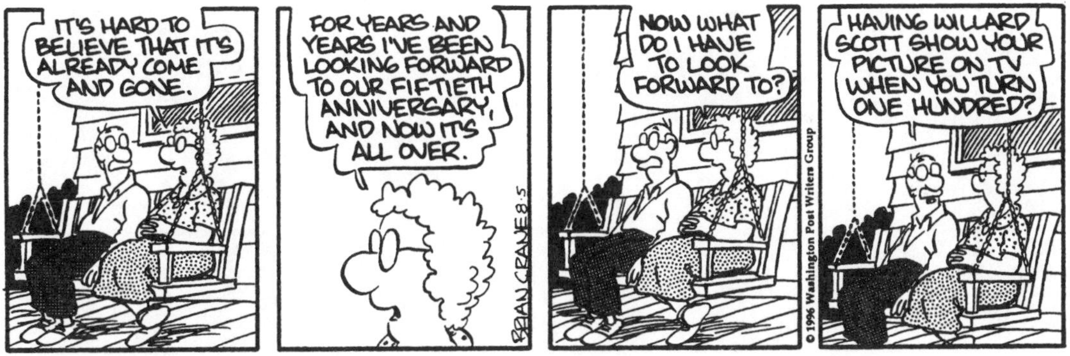

IT'S HARD TO BELIEVE THAT IT'S ALREADY COME AND GONE.
FOR YEARS AND YEARS I'VE BEEN LOOKING FORWARD TO OUR FIFTIETH ANNIVERSARY, AND NOW IT'S ALL OVER.
BRIAN CRANE 8·5
NOW WHAT DO I HAVE TO LOOK FORWARD TO?
HAVING WILLARD SCOTT SHOW YOUR PICTURE ON TV WHEN YOU TURN ONE HUNDRED?
© 1996 Washington Post Writers Group

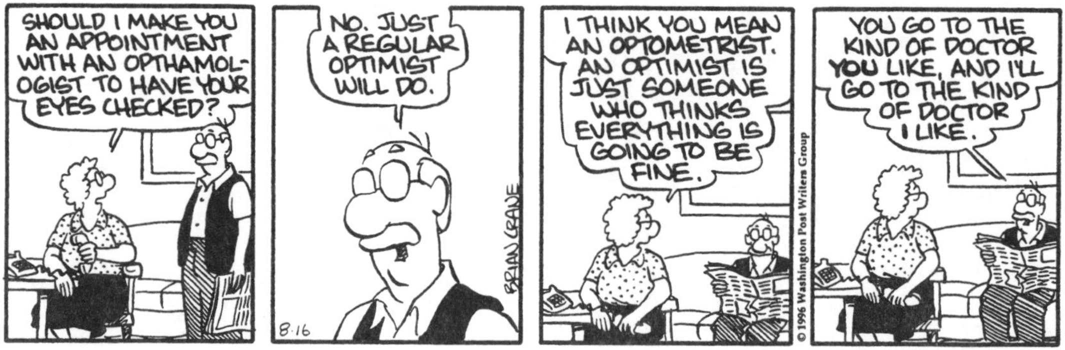
SHOULD I MAKE YOU AN APPOINTMENT WITH AN OPTHAMOLOGIST TO HAVE YOUR EYES CHECKED?
NO. JUST A REGULAR OPTIMIST WILL DO.
8·16
BRIAN CRANE
I THINK YOU MEAN AN OPTOMETRIST. AN OPTIMIST IS JUST SOMEONE WHO THINKS EVERYTHING IS GOING TO BE FINE.
© 1996 Washington Post Writers Group
YOU GO TO THE KIND OF DOCTOR YOU LIKE, AND I'LL GO TO THE KIND OF DOCTOR I LIKE.

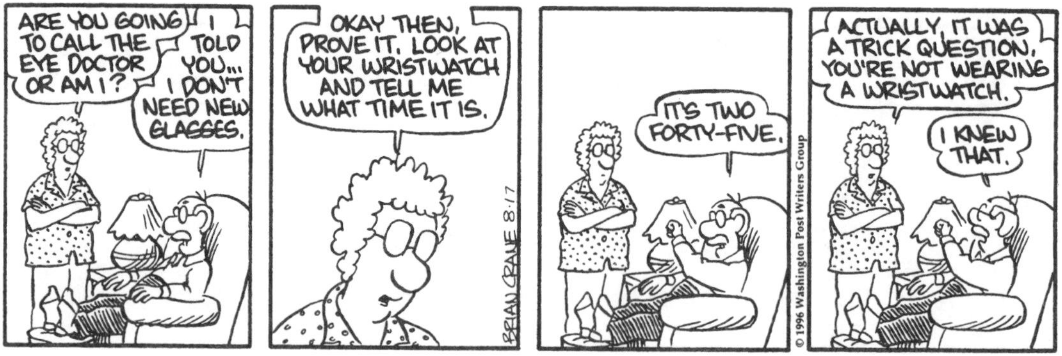
ARE YOU GOING TO CALL THE EYE DOCTOR OR AM I?
I TOLD YOU... I DON'T NEED NEW GLASSES.
OKAY THEN, PROVE IT. LOOK AT YOUR WRISTWATCH AND TELL ME WHAT TIME IT IS.
BRIAN CRANE 8·17
IT'S TWO FORTY-FIVE.
© 1996 Washington Post Writers Group
ACTUALLY, IT WAS A TRICK QUESTION. YOU'RE NOT WEARING A WRISTWATCH.
I KNEW THAT.

PICKLES

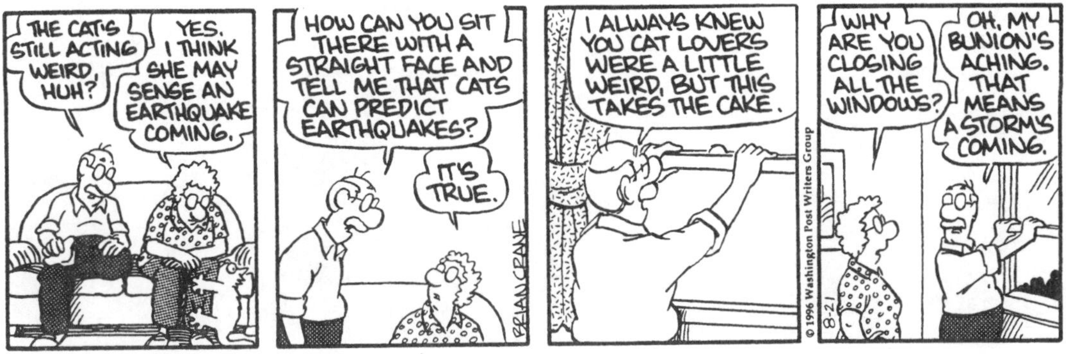

THE CAT'S STILL ACTING WEIRD, HUH?
YES. I THINK SHE MAY SENSE AN EARTHQUAKE COMING.
HOW CAN YOU SIT THERE WITH A STRAIGHT FACE AND TELL ME THAT CATS CAN PREDICT EARTHQUAKES?
IT'S TRUE.
BRIAN CRANE
I ALWAYS KNEW YOU CAT LOVERS WERE A LITTLE WEIRD, BUT THIS TAKES THE CAKE.
© 1996 Washington Post Writers Group
8-21
WHY ARE YOU CLOSING ALL THE WINDOWS?
OH, MY BUNION'S ACHING. THAT MEANS A STORM'S COMING.

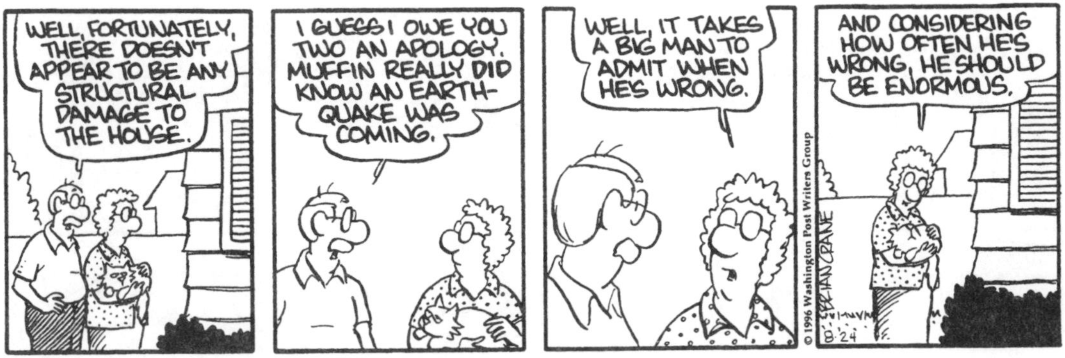

WELL, FORTUNATELY, THERE DOESN'T APPEAR TO BE ANY STRUCTURAL DAMAGE TO THE HOUSE.
I GUESS I OWE YOU TWO AN APOLOGY. MUFFIN REALLY DID KNOW AN EARTHQUAKE WAS COMING.
WELL, IT TAKES A BIG MAN TO ADMIT WHEN HE'S WRONG.
© 1996 Washington Post Writers Group
BRIAN CRANE
8-24
AND CONSIDERING HOW OFTEN HE'S WRONG, HE SHOULD BE ENORMOUS.

PICKLES

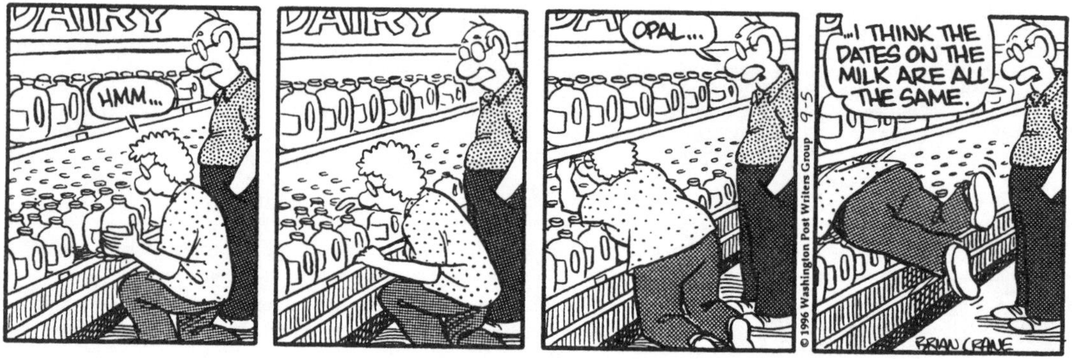
DAIRY
HMM...
OPAL...
...I THINK THE DATES ON THE MILK ARE ALL THE SAME.
© 1996 Washington Post Writers Group 9-5
BRIAN CRANE

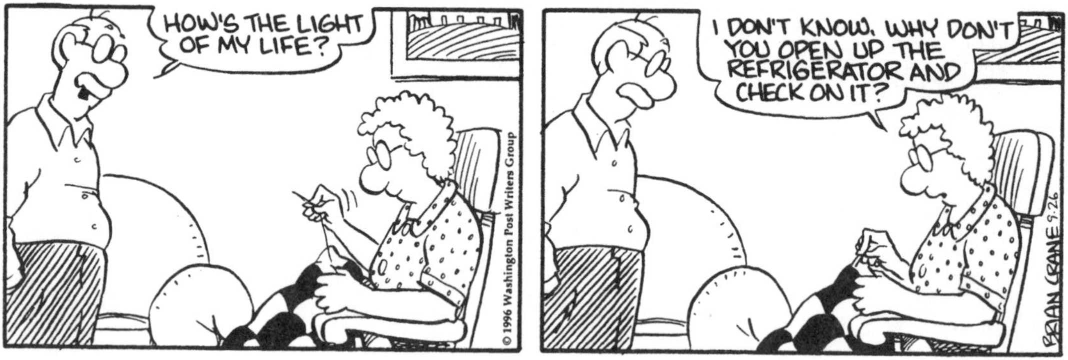
HOW'S THE LIGHT OF MY LIFE?
I DON'T KNOW. WHY DON'T YOU OPEN UP THE REFRIGERATOR AND CHECK ON IT?
© 1996 Washington Post Writers Group
BRIAN CRANE 9-26

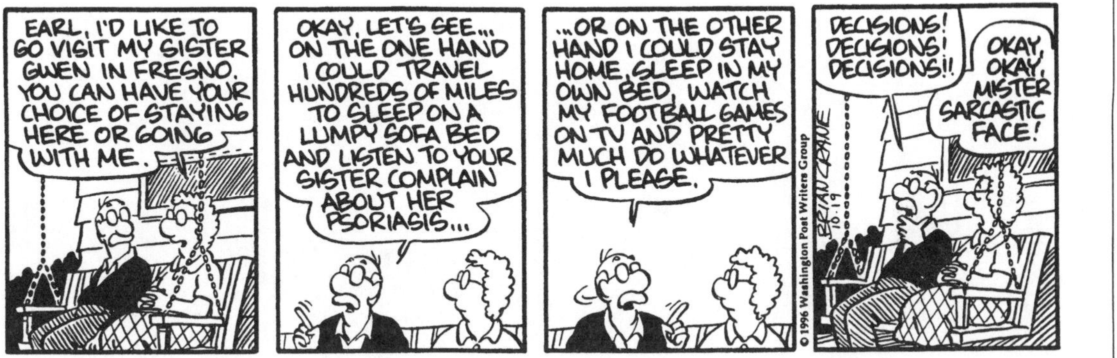
EARL, I'D LIKE TO GO VISIT MY SISTER GWEN IN FRESNO. YOU CAN HAVE YOUR CHOICE OF STAYING HERE OR GOING WITH ME.
OKAY, LET'S SEE... ON THE ONE HAND I COULD TRAVEL HUNDREDS OF MILES TO SLEEP ON A LUMPY SOFA BED AND LISTEN TO YOUR SISTER COMPLAIN ABOUT HER PSORIASIS...
...OR ON THE OTHER HAND I COULD STAY HOME, SLEEP IN MY OWN BED, WATCH MY FOOTBALL GAMES ON TV AND PRETTY MUCH DO WHATEVER I PLEASE.
© 1996 Washington Post Writers Group
BRIAN CRANE 10·19
DECISIONS! DECISIONS! DECISIONS!!
OKAY, OKAY, MISTER SARCASTIC FACE!

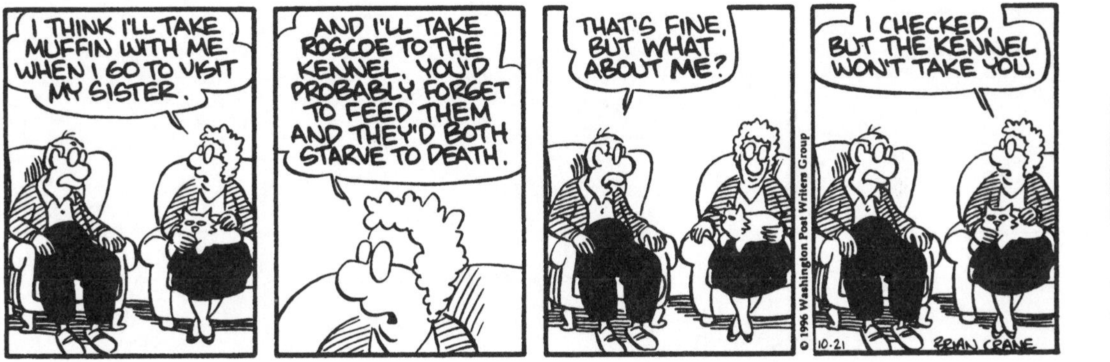
I THINK I'LL TAKE MUFFIN WITH ME WHEN I GO TO VISIT MY SISTER.
AND I'LL TAKE ROSCOE TO THE KENNEL. YOU'D PROBABLY FORGET TO FEED THEM AND THEY'D BOTH STARVE TO DEATH.
THAT'S FINE, BUT WHAT ABOUT ME?
© 1996 Washington Post Writers Group
I CHECKED, BUT THE KENNEL WON'T TAKE YOU.
10·21
BRIAN CRANE

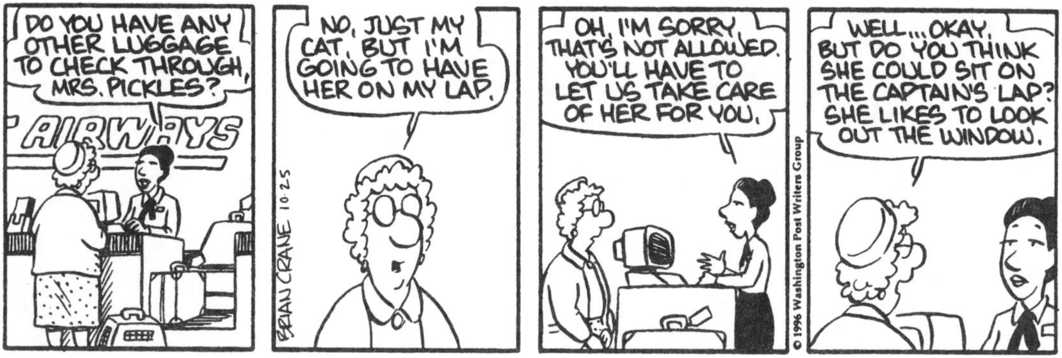
DO YOU HAVE ANY OTHER LUGGAGE TO CHECK THROUGH, MRS. PICKLES?
AIRWAYS
NO, JUST MY CAT, BUT I'M GOING TO HAVE HER ON MY LAP.
BRIAN CRANE 10·25
OH, I'M SORRY, THAT'S NOT ALLOWED. YOU'LL HAVE TO LET US TAKE CARE OF HER FOR YOU.
© 1996 Washington Post Writers Group
WELL...OKAY. BUT DO YOU THINK SHE COULD SIT ON THE CAPTAIN'S LAP? SHE LIKES TO LOOK OUT THE WINDOW.

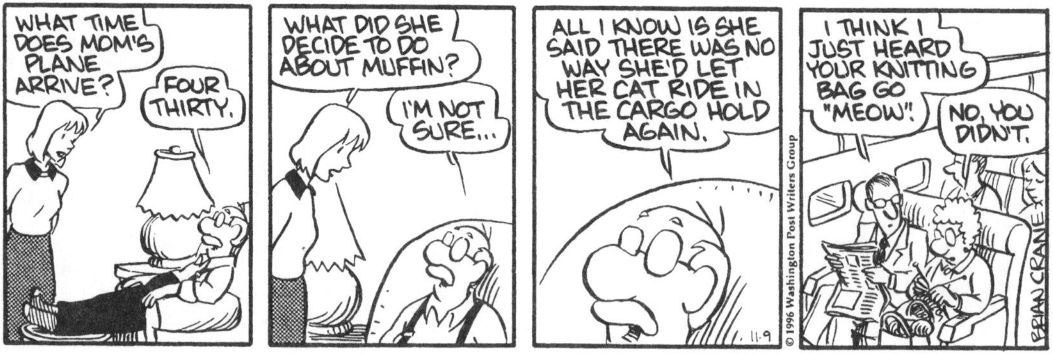
WHAT TIME DOES MOM'S PLANE ARRIVE?
FOUR THIRTY.
WHAT DID SHE DECIDE TO DO ABOUT MUFFIN?
I'M NOT SURE...
ALL I KNOW IS SHE SAID THERE WAS NO WAY SHE'D LET HER CAT RIDE IN THE CARGO HOLD AGAIN.
11·9
© 1996 Washington Post Writers Group
I THINK I JUST HEARD YOUR KNITTING BAG GO "MEOW".
NO, YOU DIDN'T.
BRIAN CRANE

PICKLES

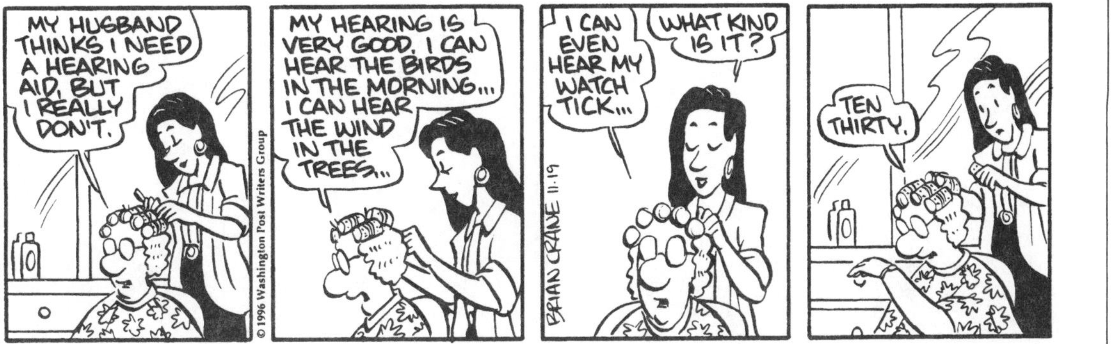
MY HUSBAND THINKS I NEED A HEARING AID, BUT I REALLY DON'T.
MY HEARING IS VERY GOOD. I CAN HEAR THE BIRDS IN THE MORNING... I CAN HEAR THE WIND IN THE TREES...
© 1996 Washington Post Writers Group
BRIAN CRANE 11-19
I CAN EVEN HEAR MY WATCH TICK...
WHAT KIND IS IT?
TEN THIRTY.

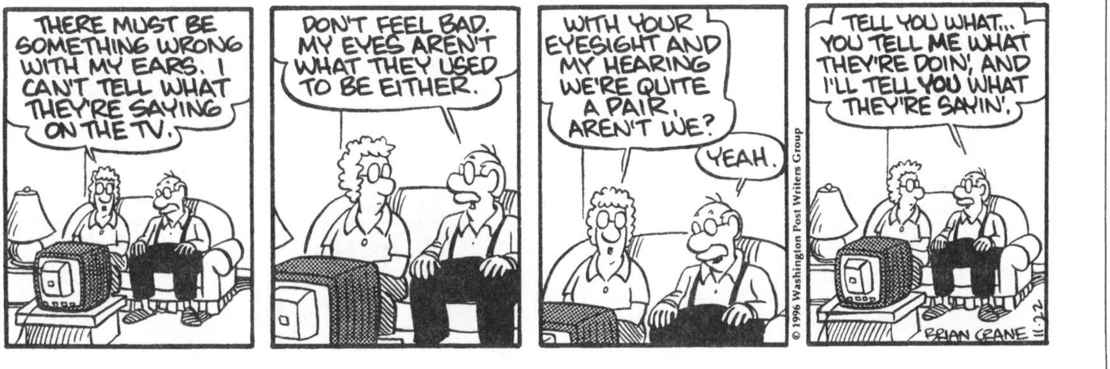
THERE MUST BE SOMETHING WRONG WITH MY EARS. I CAN'T TELL WHAT THEY'RE SAYING ON THE TV.
DON'T FEEL BAD. MY EYES AREN'T WHAT THEY USED TO BE EITHER.
WITH YOUR EYESIGHT AND MY HEARING WE'RE QUITE A PAIR, AREN'T WE?
YEAH.
© 1996 Washington Post Writers Group
TELL YOU WHAT... YOU TELL ME WHAT THEY'RE DOIN', AND I'LL TELL YOU WHAT THEY'RE SAYIN'.
BRIAN CRANE 11-22

YOU WANT SOMETHING TO EAT?
DEPENDS...
WHAT ARE MY CHOICES?
YES OR NO.
BRIAN CRANE 11-25
© 1996 Washington Post Writers Group

THIS WIND'S REALLY HARD ON THE HAIR.
I GUESS YOU DON'T HAVE THAT PROBLEM, THOUGH, DO YOU?
YOU KNOW WHAT THEY SAY... GRASS DOESN'T GROW ON A BUSY STREET.
WELL, I ALWAYS SAY THERE'S NO SENSE PUTTIN' A ROOF ON AN EMPTY SHED.
BRIAN CRANE 12-28
© 1996 Washington Post Writers Group

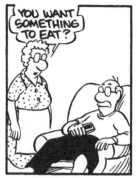

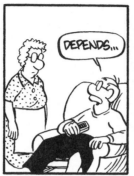

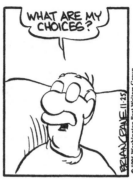

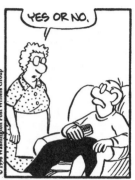

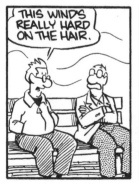

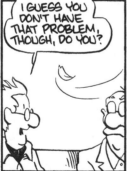

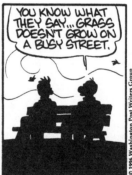

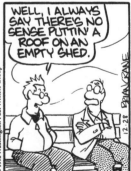

PICKLES

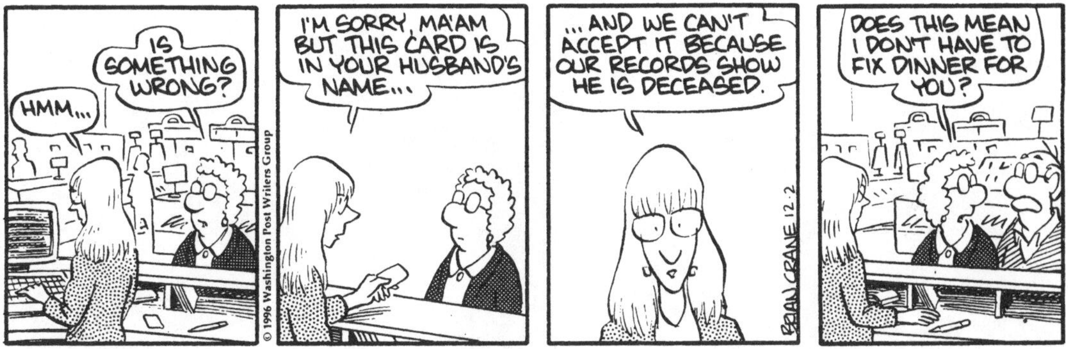
HMM...
IS SOMETHING WRONG?
I'M SORRY, MA'AM BUT THIS CARD IS IN YOUR HUSBAND'S NAME...
...AND WE CAN'T ACCEPT IT BECAUSE OUR RECORDS SHOW HE IS DECEASED.
DOES THIS MEAN I DON'T HAVE TO FIX DINNER FOR YOU?
© 1996 Washington Post Writers Group
BRIAN CRANE 12·2

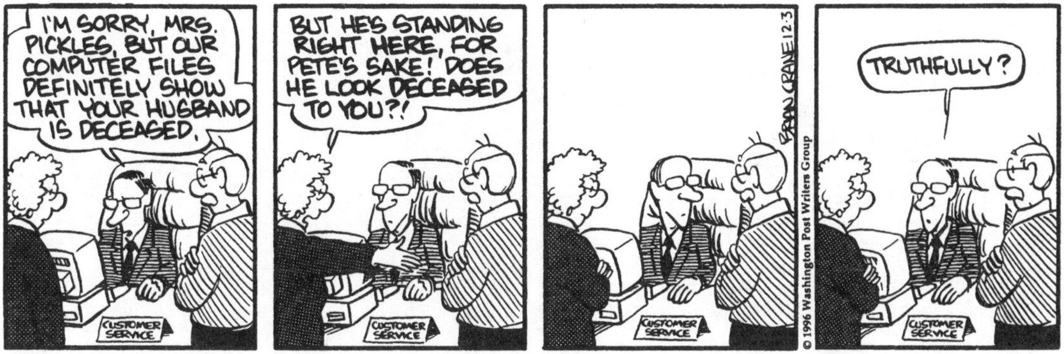
I'M SORRY, MRS. PICKLES, BUT OUR COMPUTER FILES DEFINITELY SHOW THAT YOUR HUSBAND IS DECEASED.
CUSTOMER SERVICE
BUT HE'S STANDING RIGHT HERE, FOR PETE'S SAKE! DOES HE LOOK DECEASED TO YOU?!
BRIAN CRANE 12·3
© 1996 Washington Post Writers Group
TRUTHFULLY?

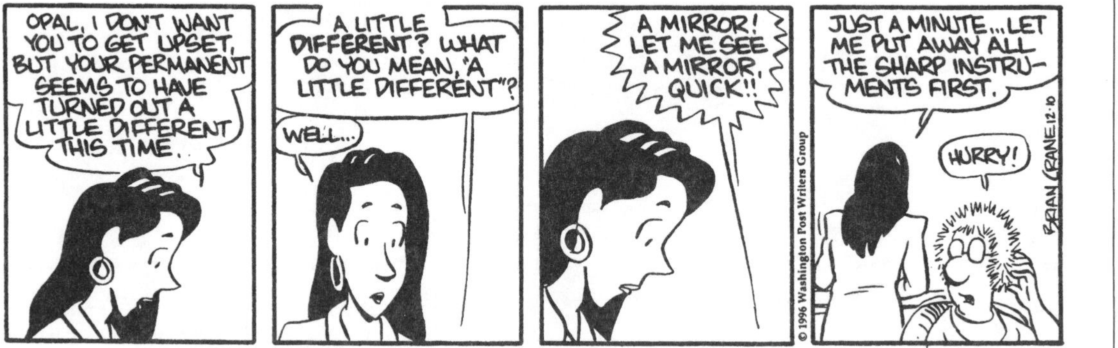
OPAL, I DON'T WANT YOU TO GET UPSET, BUT YOUR PERMANENT SEEMS TO HAVE TURNED OUT A LITTLE DIFFERENT THIS TIME...
A LITTLE DIFFERENT? WHAT DO YOU MEAN, "A LITTLE DIFFERENT"?
WELL...
A MIRROR! LET ME SEE A MIRROR, QUICK!!
JUST A MINUTE...LET ME PUT AWAY ALL THE SHARP INSTRUMENTS FIRST.
HURRY!
© 1996 Washington Post Writers Group
BRIAN CRANE 12·10

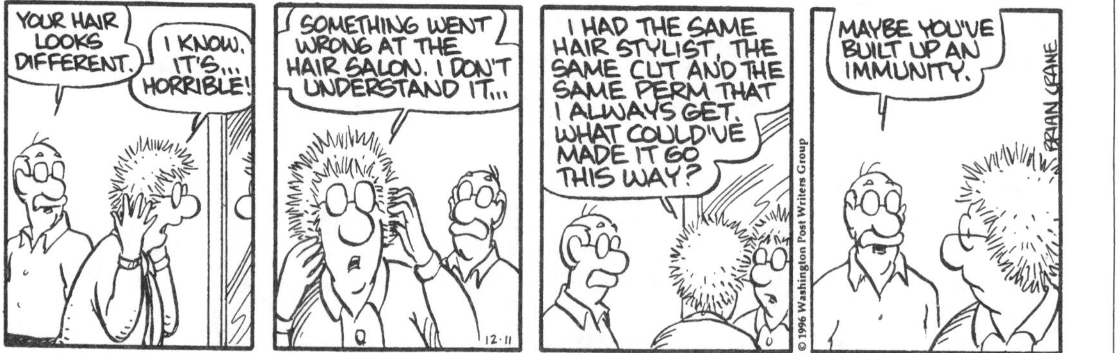
YOUR HAIR LOOKS DIFFERENT.
I KNOW. IT'S... HORRIBLE!
SOMETHING WENT WRONG AT THE HAIR SALON. I DON'T UNDERSTAND IT...
12·11
I HAD THE SAME HAIR STYLIST, THE SAME CUT AND THE SAME PERM THAT I ALWAYS GET. WHAT COULD'VE MADE IT GO THIS WAY?
© 1996 Washington Post Writers Group
MAYBE YOU'VE BUILT UP AN IMMUNITY.
BRIAN CRANE

PICKLES

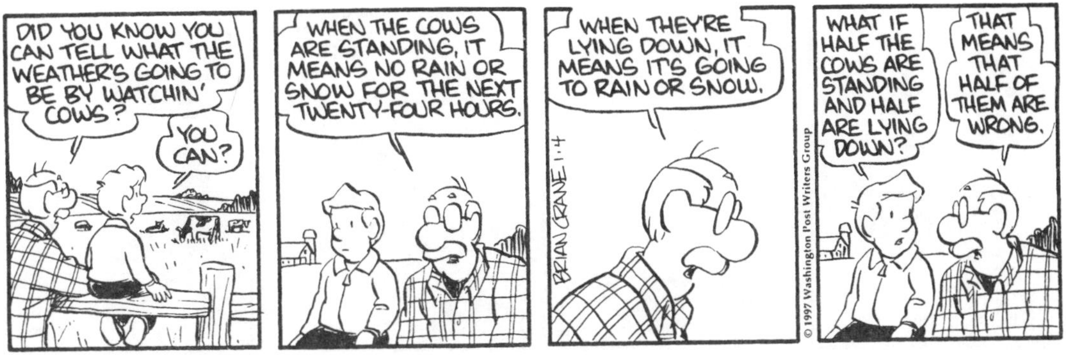
DID YOU KNOW YOU CAN TELL WHAT THE WEATHER'S GOING TO BE BY WATCHIN' COWS?
YOU CAN?
WHEN THE COWS ARE STANDING, IT MEANS NO RAIN OR SNOW FOR THE NEXT TWENTY-FOUR HOURS.
WHEN THEY'RE LYING DOWN, IT MEANS IT'S GOING TO RAIN OR SNOW.
BRIAN CRANE 1-4
WHAT IF HALF THE COWS ARE STANDING AND HALF ARE LYING DOWN?
THAT MEANS THAT HALF OF THEM ARE WRONG.
© 1997 Washington Post Writers Group

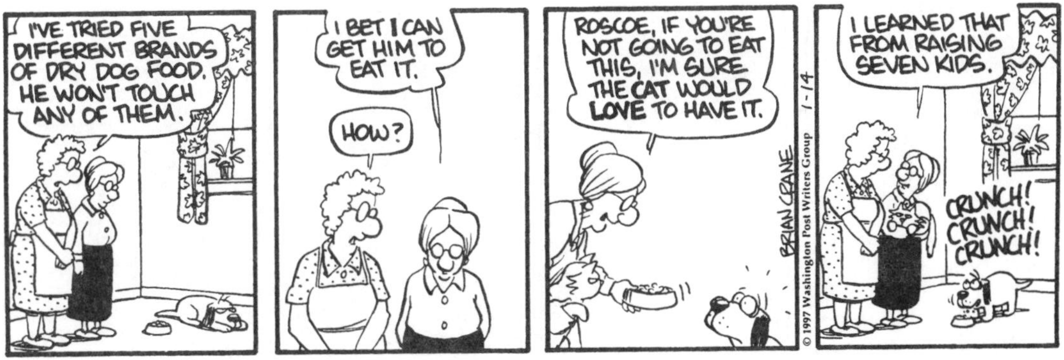
I'VE TRIED FIVE DIFFERENT BRANDS OF DRY DOG FOOD. HE WON'T TOUCH ANY OF THEM.
I BET I CAN GET HIM TO EAT IT.
HOW?
ROSCOE, IF YOU'RE NOT GOING TO EAT THIS, I'M SURE THE CAT WOULD LOVE TO HAVE IT.
BRIAN CRANE 1-14
© 1997 Washington Post Writers Group
I LEARNED THAT FROM RAISING SEVEN KIDS.
CRUNCH! CRUNCH! CRUNCH!

PICKLES

WHY ARE WE STOPPING?
THE OLD STUDEBAKER JUST TURNED 200,000 MILES. I WANT TO GET A PICTURE OF THE ODOMETER.
HOW COME YOU NEVER TAKE ANY PICTURES OF ME?
WELL, WITH THE PRICE OF FILM NOWADAYS I HAVE TO BE VERY SELECTIVE.
© 1997 Washington Post Writers Group
WHAT? DID I SAY SOMETHING WRONG?
BRIAN CRANE 1-30

I'M SORRY TO BE HARD-NOSED ABOUT THIS, BUT I CAN'T TAKE LIVING WITH ANOTHER CAT. ONE IS ENOUGH.
EITHER THE KITTEN GOES OR I GO.
BRIAN CRANE
WELL? WHAT'S IT GOING TO BE?
© 1997 Washington Post Writers Group
I'M THINKING, I'M THINKING...

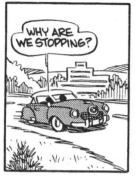

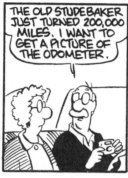

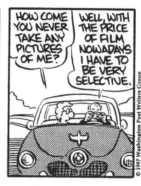

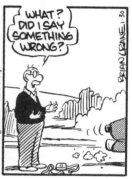

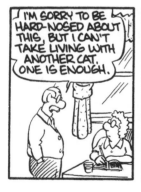

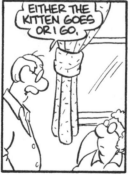

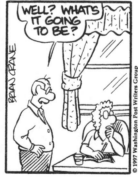

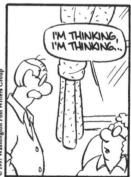

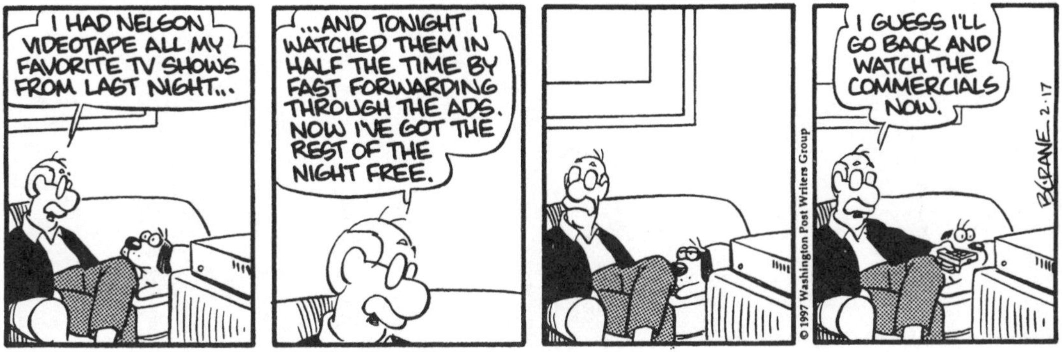
I HAD NELSON VIDEOTAPE ALL MY FAVORITE TV SHOWS FROM LAST NIGHT...
...AND TONIGHT I WATCHED THEM IN HALF THE TIME BY FAST FORWARDING THROUGH THE ADS. NOW I'VE GOT THE REST OF THE NIGHT FREE.
I GUESS I'LL GO BACK AND WATCH THE COMMERCIALS NOW.
© 1997 Washington Post Writers Group
B. CRANE 2·17

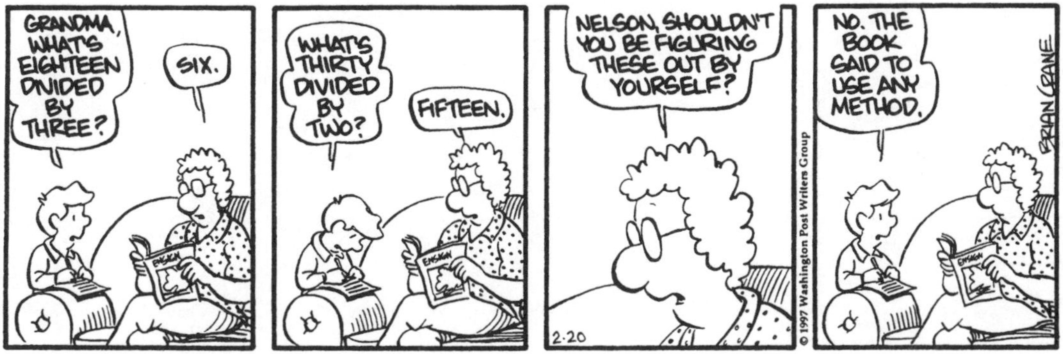
GRANDMA, WHAT'S EIGHTEEN DIVIDED BY THREE?
SIX.
WHAT'S THIRTY DIVIDED BY TWO?
FIFTEEN.
NELSON, SHOULDN'T YOU BE FIGURING THESE OUT BY YOURSELF?
2·20
NO. THE BOOK SAID TO USE ANY METHOD.
© 1997 Washington Post Writers Group
BRIAN CRANE

PICKLES

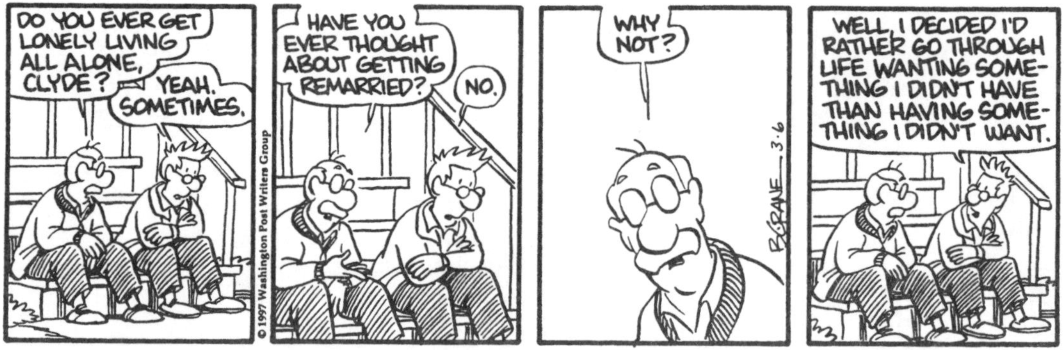
DO YOU EVER GET LONELY LIVING ALL ALONE, CLYDE?
YEAH. SOMETIMES.
© 1997 Washington Post Writers Group
HAVE YOU EVER THOUGHT ABOUT GETTING REMARRIED?
NO.
WHY NOT?
B.CRANE 3·6
WELL, I DECIDED I'D RATHER GO THROUGH LIFE WANTING SOMETHING I DIDN'T HAVE THAN HAVING SOMETHING I DIDN'T WANT.

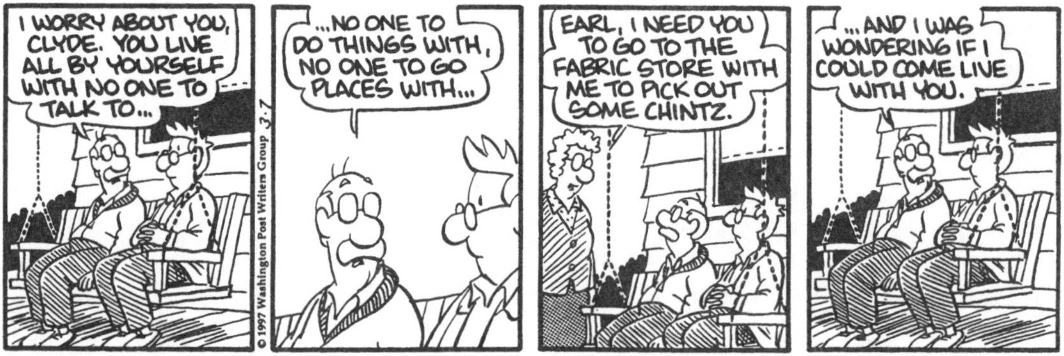
I WORRY ABOUT YOU, CLYDE. YOU LIVE ALL BY YOURSELF WITH NO ONE TO TALK TO...
© 1997 Washington Post Writers Group 3·7
...NO ONE TO DO THINGS WITH, NO ONE TO GO PLACES WITH...
EARL, I NEED YOU TO GO TO THE FABRIC STORE WITH ME TO PICK OUT SOME CHINTZ.
...AND I WAS WONDERING IF I COULD COME LIVE WITH YOU.

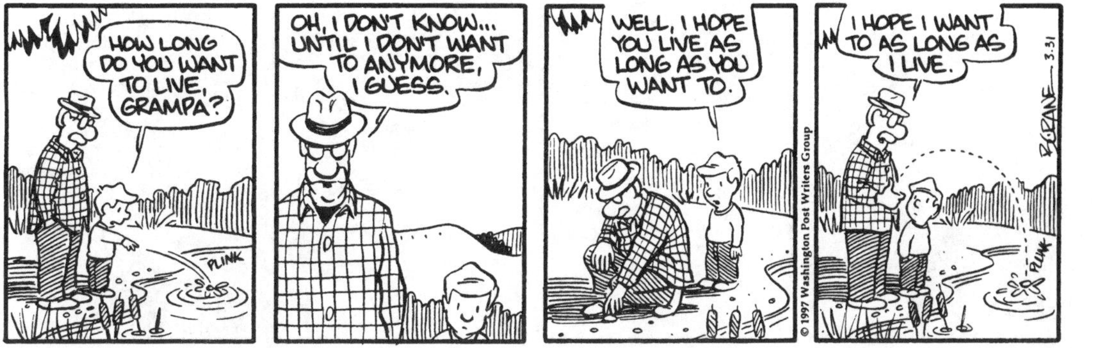
HOW LONG DO YOU WANT TO LIVE, GRAMPA?
PLINK
OH, I DON'T KNOW... UNTIL I DON'T WANT TO ANYMORE, I GUESS.
WELL, I HOPE YOU LIVE AS LONG AS YOU WANT TO.
© 1997 Washington Post Writers Group
I HOPE I WANT TO AS LONG AS I LIVE.
3.31
B. CRANE
PLINK

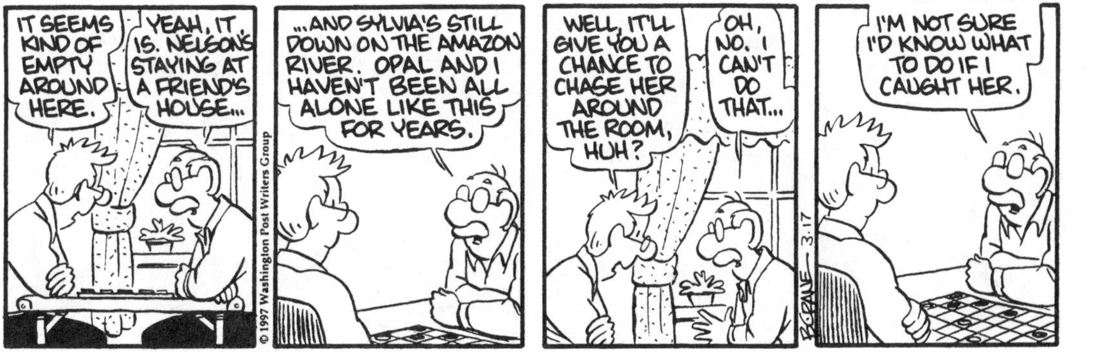
IT SEEMS KIND OF EMPTY AROUND HERE.
YEAH, IT IS. NELSON'S STAYING AT A FRIEND'S HOUSE...
© 1997 Washington Post Writers Group
...AND SYLVIA'S STILL DOWN ON THE AMAZON RIVER. OPAL AND I HAVEN'T BEEN ALL ALONE LIKE THIS FOR YEARS.
WELL, IT'LL GIVE YOU A CHANCE TO CHASE HER AROUND THE ROOM, HUH?
OH, NO. I CAN'T DO THAT...
3.17
B. CRANE
I'M NOT SURE I'D KNOW WHAT TO DO IF I CAUGHT HER.

PICKLES

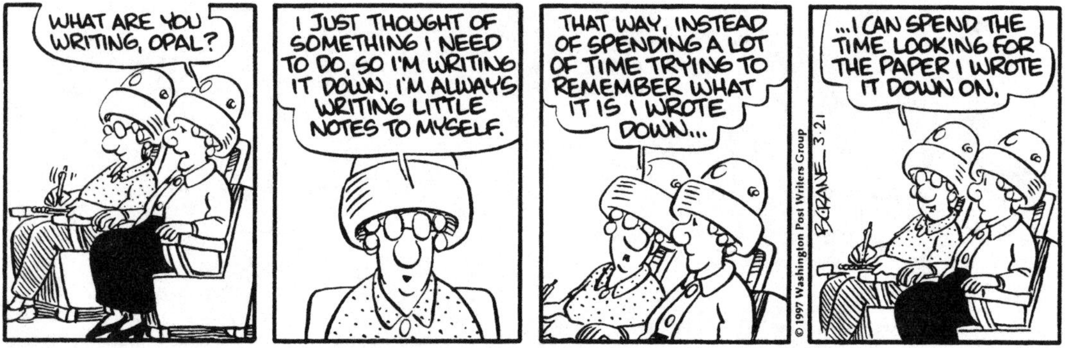
WHAT ARE YOU WRITING, OPAL?
I JUST THOUGHT OF SOMETHING I NEED TO DO, SO I'M WRITING IT DOWN. I'M ALWAYS WRITING LITTLE NOTES TO MYSELF.
THAT WAY, INSTEAD OF SPENDING A LOT OF TIME TRYING TO REMEMBER WHAT IT IS I WROTE DOWN...
© 1997 Washington Post Writers Group
B. CRANE 3·21
...I CAN SPEND THE TIME LOOKING FOR THE PAPER I WROTE IT DOWN ON.

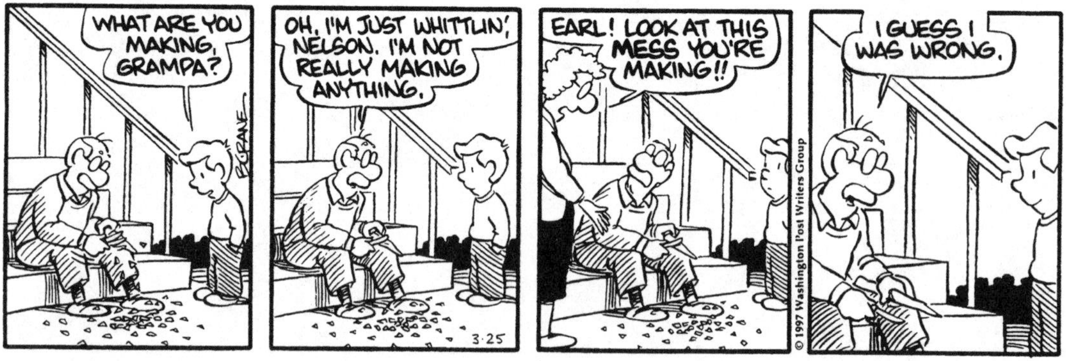
WHAT ARE YOU MAKING, GRAMPA?
B. CRANE
OH, I'M JUST WHITTLIN', NELSON. I'M NOT REALLY MAKING ANYTHING.
3·25
EARL! LOOK AT THIS MESS YOU'RE MAKING!!
© 1997 Washington Post Writers Group
I GUESS I WAS WRONG.

GIVE ME $30. I'M TAKING ROSCOE TO THE GROOMER FOR A BATH.
WHY? I CAN GIVE HIM A BATH.
THEY ALSO CLIP HIS FUR.
I CAN DO THAT TOO.
...AND THEY CLEAN OUT HIS ANAL GLANDS.
© 1997 Washington Post Writers Group
HERE'S $40. GIVE 'EM A BIG TIP.

IF YOU'RE TIRED, I'LL TAKE HIM FOR A WALK.
NO THANKS. I'M FINE.
© 1997 Washington Post Writers Group
I WAS TALKIN' TO THE DOG.

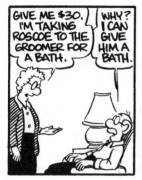

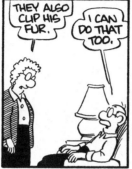

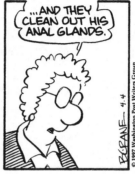

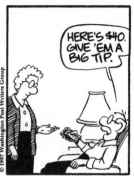

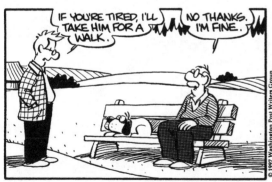

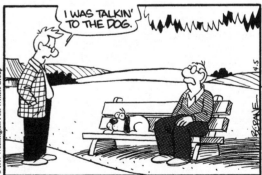

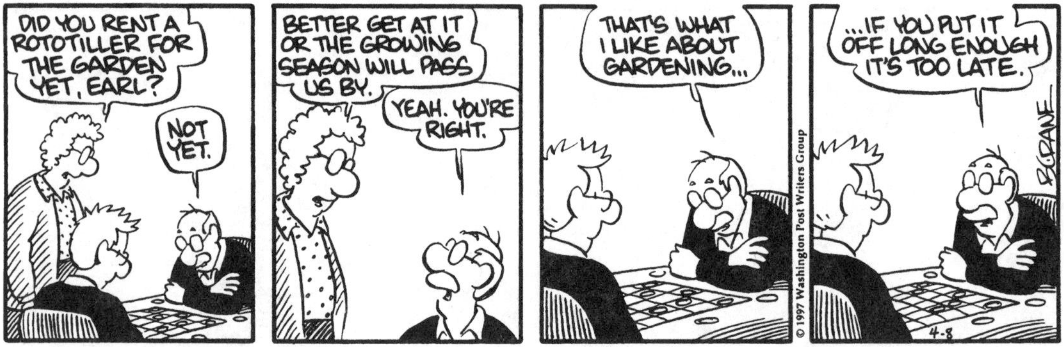
DID YOU RENT A ROTOTILLER FOR THE GARDEN YET, EARL?
NOT YET.
BETTER GET AT IT OR THE GROWING SEASON WILL PASS US BY.
YEAH. YOU'RE RIGHT.
THAT'S WHAT I LIKE ABOUT GARDENING...
...IF YOU PUT IT OFF LONG ENOUGH IT'S TOO LATE.
© 1997 Washington Post Writers Group
B. CRANE
4-8

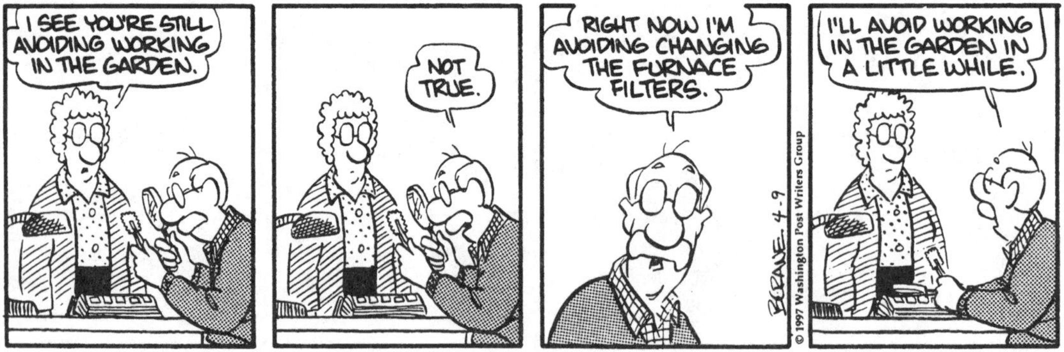
I SEE YOU'RE STILL AVOIDING WORKING IN THE GARDEN.
NOT TRUE.
RIGHT NOW I'M AVOIDING CHANGING THE FURNACE FILTERS.
I'LL AVOID WORKING IN THE GARDEN IN A LITTLE WHILE.
© 1997 Washington Post Writers Group
B. CRANE 4-9

PICKLES

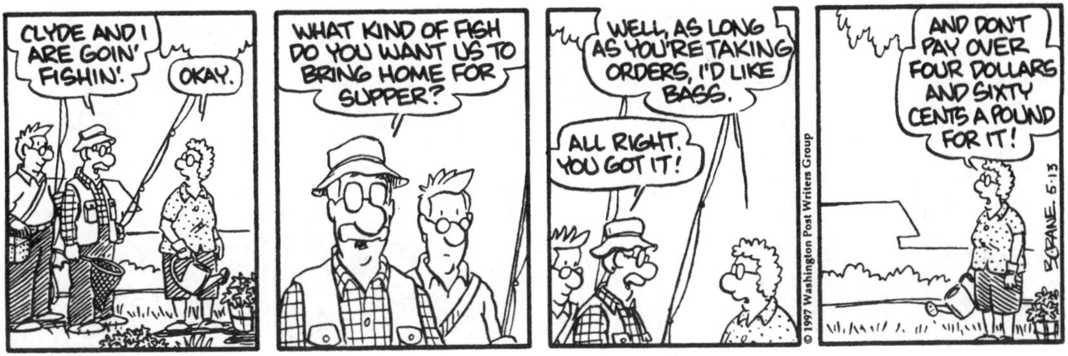
CLYDE AND I ARE GOIN' FISHIN'.
OKAY.
WHAT KIND OF FISH DO YOU WANT US TO BRING HOME FOR SUPPER?
WELL, AS LONG AS YOU'RE TAKING ORDERS, I'D LIKE BASS.
ALL RIGHT. YOU GOT IT!
© 1997 Washington Post Writers Group
AND DON'T PAY OVER FOUR DOLLARS AND SIXTY CENTS A POUND FOR IT!
B. CRANE 5·13

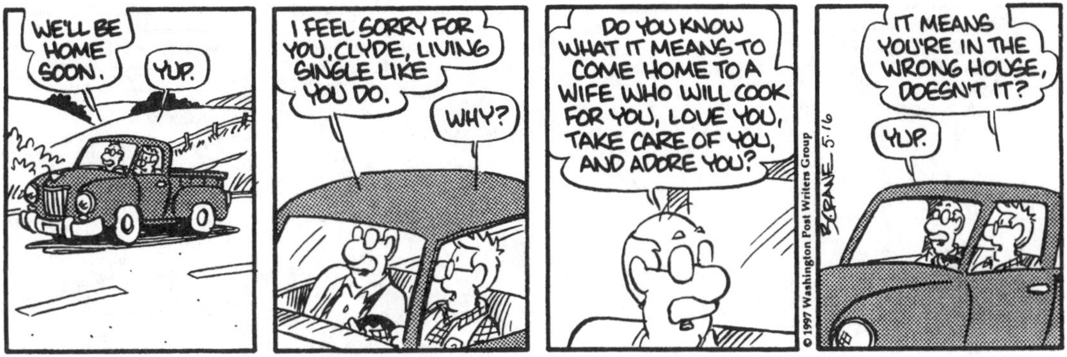
WE'LL BE HOME SOON.
YUP.
I FEEL SORRY FOR YOU, CLYDE, LIVING SINGLE LIKE YOU DO.
WHY?
DO YOU KNOW WHAT IT MEANS TO COME HOME TO A WIFE WHO WILL COOK FOR YOU, LOVE YOU, TAKE CARE OF YOU, AND ADORE YOU?
© 1997 Washington Post Writers Group
B. CRANE 5·16
IT MEANS YOU'RE IN THE WRONG HOUSE, DOESN'T IT?
YUP.

PICKLES

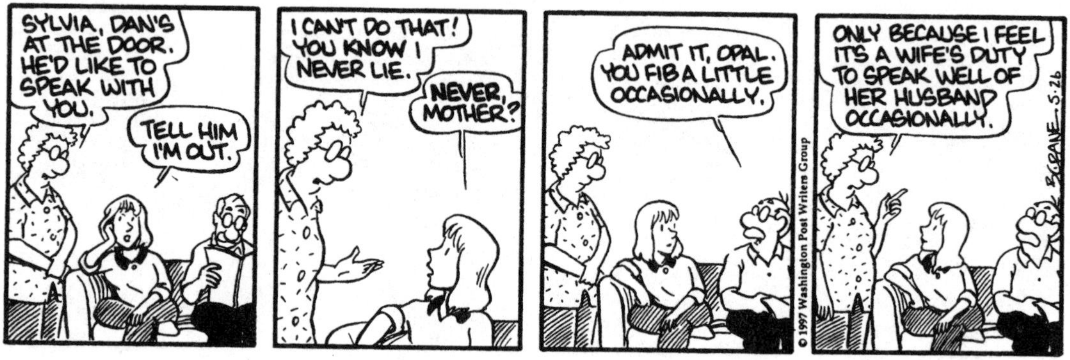
SYLVIA, DAN'S AT THE DOOR. HE'D LIKE TO SPEAK WITH YOU.
TELL HIM I'M OUT.
I CAN'T DO THAT! YOU KNOW I NEVER LIE.
NEVER, MOTHER?
ADMIT IT, OPAL. YOU FIB A LITTLE OCCASIONALLY.
ONLY BECAUSE I FEEL IT'S A WIFE'S DUTY TO SPEAK WELL OF HER HUSBAND OCCASIONALLY.
© 1997 Washington Post Writers Group
B. CRANE 5·26

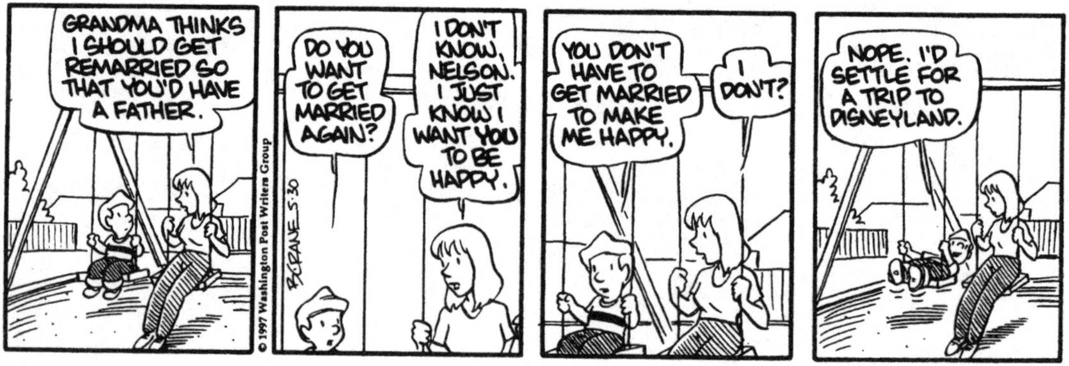
GRANDMA THINKS I SHOULD GET REMARRIED SO THAT YOU'D HAVE A FATHER.
© 1997 Washington Post Writers Group
DO YOU WANT TO GET MARRIED AGAIN?
I DON'T KNOW, NELSON. I JUST KNOW I WANT YOU TO BE HAPPY.
B. CRANE 5·30
YOU DON'T HAVE TO GET MARRIED TO MAKE ME HAPPY.
I DON'T?
NOPE. I'D SETTLE FOR A TRIP TO DISNEYLAND.

PICKLES

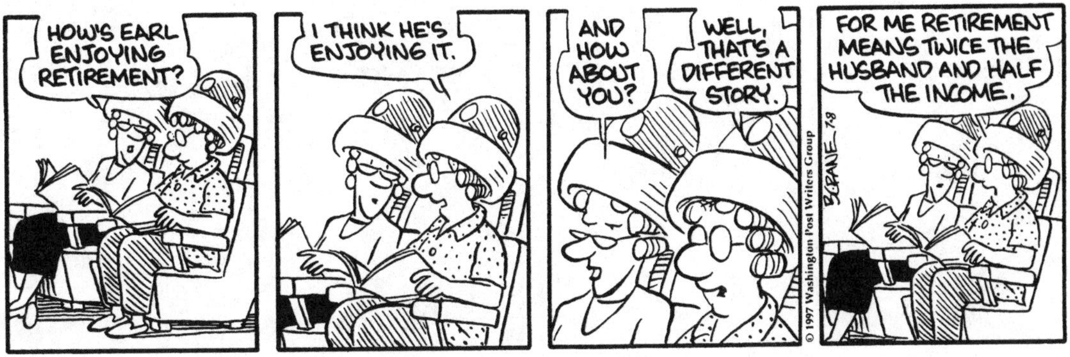
HOW'S EARL ENJOYING RETIREMENT?
I THINK HE'S ENJOYING IT.
AND HOW ABOUT YOU?
WELL, THAT'S A DIFFERENT STORY.
© 1997 Washington Post Writers Group
FOR ME RETIREMENT MEANS TWICE THE HUSBAND AND HALF THE INCOME.

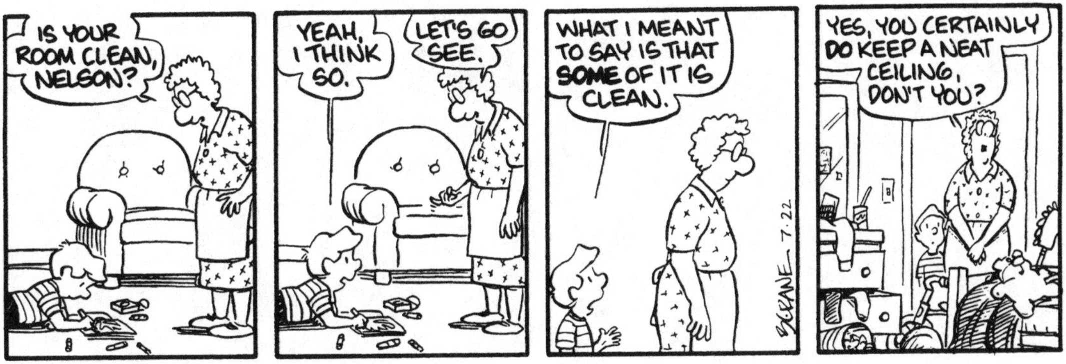
IS YOUR ROOM CLEAN, NELSON?
YEAH, I THINK SO.
LET'S GO SEE.
WHAT I MEANT TO SAY IS THAT SOME OF IT IS CLEAN.
YES, YOU CERTAINLY DO KEEP A NEAT CEILING, DON'T YOU?

PICKLES

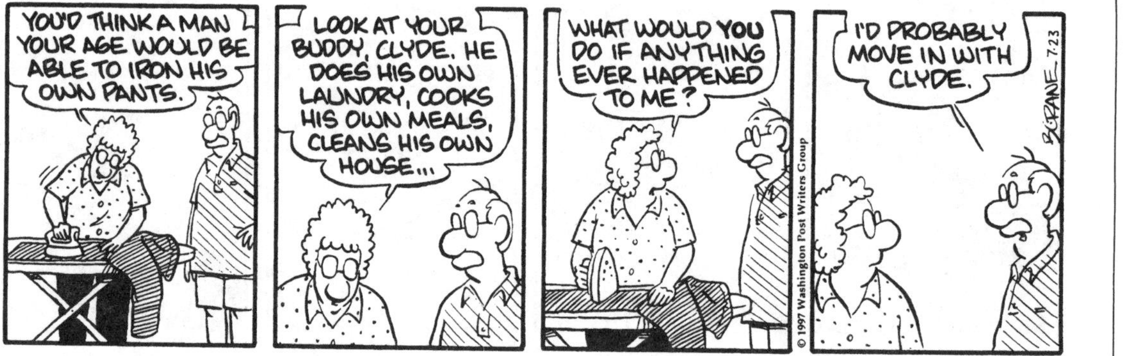
YOU'D THINK A MAN YOUR AGE WOULD BE ABLE TO IRON HIS OWN PANTS.
LOOK AT YOUR BUDDY, CLYDE. HE DOES HIS OWN LAUNDRY, COOKS HIS OWN MEALS, CLEANS HIS OWN HOUSE...
WHAT WOULD YOU DO IF ANYTHING EVER HAPPENED TO ME?
I'D PROBABLY MOVE IN WITH CLYDE.
© 1997 Washington Post Writers Group
B. CRANE 7·23

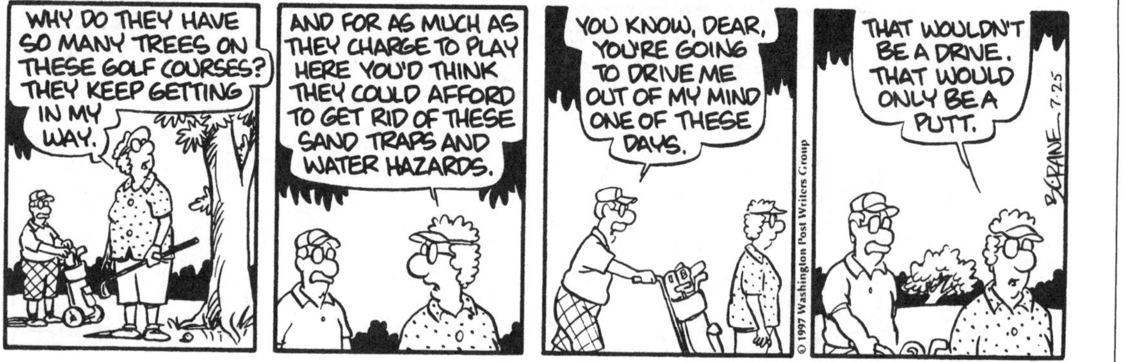
WHY DO THEY HAVE SO MANY TREES ON THESE GOLF COURSES? THEY KEEP GETTING IN MY WAY.
AND FOR AS MUCH AS THEY CHARGE TO PLAY HERE YOU'D THINK THEY COULD AFFORD TO GET RID OF THESE SAND TRAPS AND WATER HAZARDS.
YOU KNOW, DEAR, YOU'RE GOING TO DRIVE ME OUT OF MY MIND ONE OF THESE DAYS.
THAT WOULDN'T BE A DRIVE. THAT WOULD ONLY BE A PUTT.
© 1997 Washington Post Writers Group
B. CRANE 7·25

PICKLES

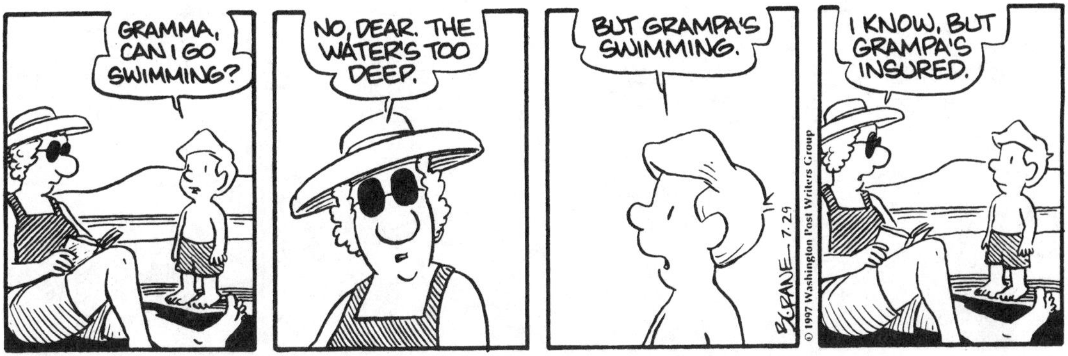
GRAMMA, CAN I GO SWIMMING?
NO, DEAR. THE WATER'S TOO DEEP.
BUT GRAMPA'S SWIMMING.
I KNOW, BUT GRAMPA'S INSURED.
B.CRANE 7.29
© 1997 Washington Post Writers Group

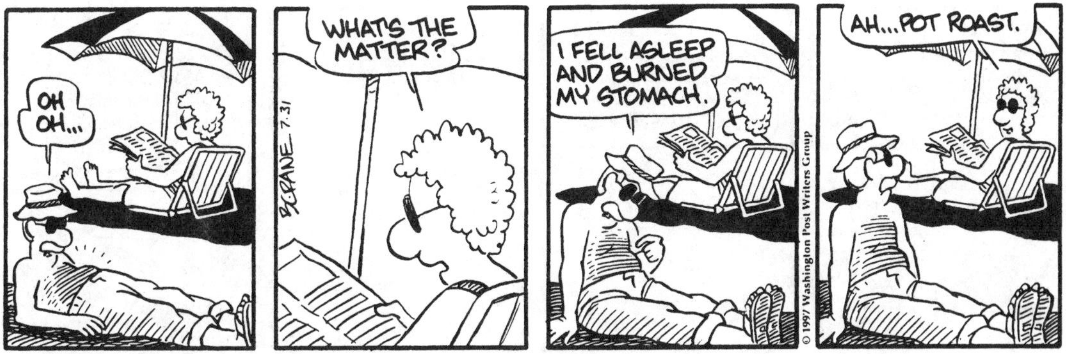
OH OH...
WHAT'S THE MATTER?
I FELL ASLEEP AND BURNED MY STOMACH.
AH...POT ROAST.
B.CRANE 7.31
© 1997 Washington Post Writers Group

PICKLES

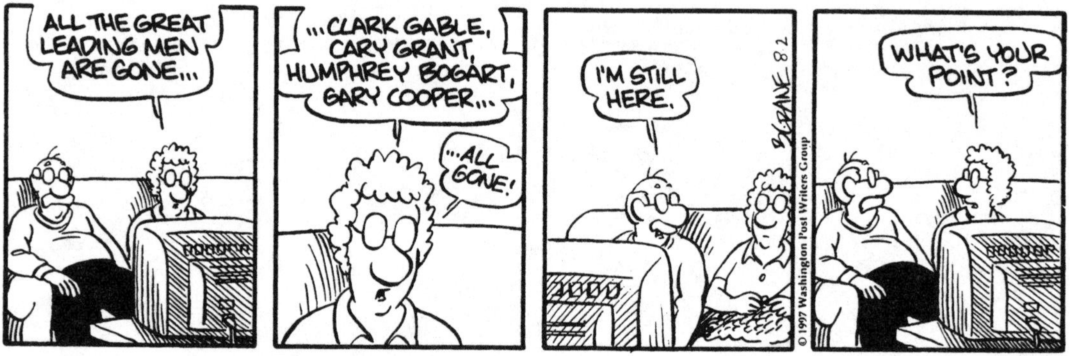
ALL THE GREAT LEADING MEN ARE GONE...
...CLARK GABLE, CARY GRANT, HUMPHREY BOGART, GARY COOPER...
...ALL GONE!
I'M STILL HERE.
B.CRANE 8-2
© 1997 Washington Post Writers Group
WHAT'S YOUR POINT?

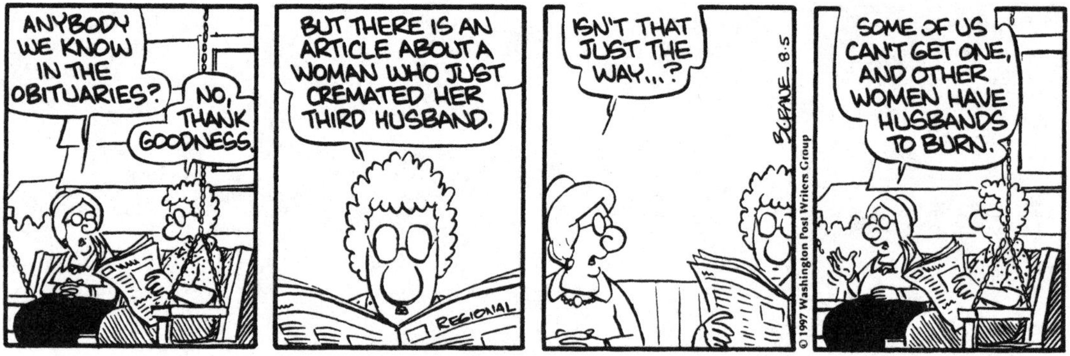
ANYBODY WE KNOW IN THE OBITUARIES?
NO, THANK GOODNESS.
BUT THERE IS AN ARTICLE ABOUT A WOMAN WHO JUST CREMATED HER THIRD HUSBAND.
REGIONAL
ISN'T THAT JUST THE WAY...?
B.CRANE 8-5
© 1997 Washington Post Writers Group
SOME OF US CAN'T GET ONE, AND OTHER WOMEN HAVE HUSBANDS TO BURN.

PICKLES

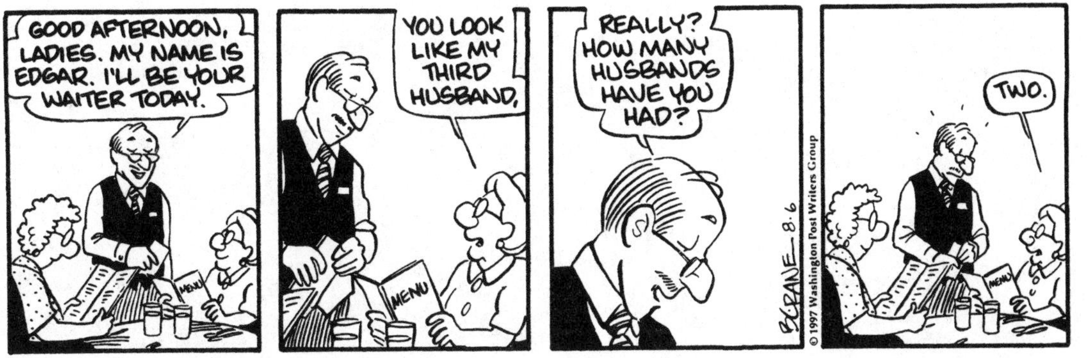

GOOD AFTERNOON, LADIES. MY NAME IS EDGAR. I'LL BE YOUR WAITER TODAY.
MENU
YOU LOOK LIKE MY THIRD HUSBAND.
MENU
REALLY? HOW MANY HUSBANDS HAVE YOU HAD?
B. CRANE 8-6
© 1997 Washington Post Writers Group
TWO.
MENU

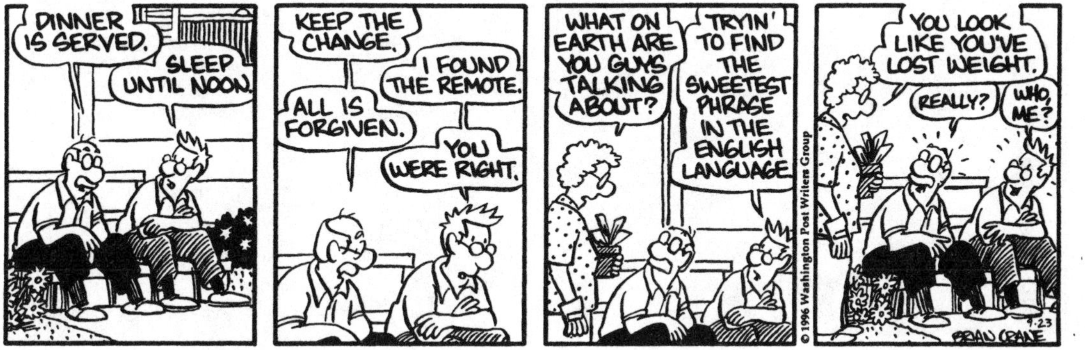

DINNER IS SERVED.
SLEEP UNTIL NOON.
KEEP THE CHANGE.
I FOUND THE REMOTE.
ALL IS FORGIVEN.
YOU WERE RIGHT.
WHAT ON EARTH ARE YOU GUYS TALKING ABOUT?
TRYIN' TO FIND THE SWEETEST PHRASE IN THE ENGLISH LANGUAGE.
© 1996 Washington Post Writers Group
YOU LOOK LIKE YOU'VE LOST WEIGHT.
REALLY?
WHO, ME?
9-23
BRIAN CRANE

PICKLES

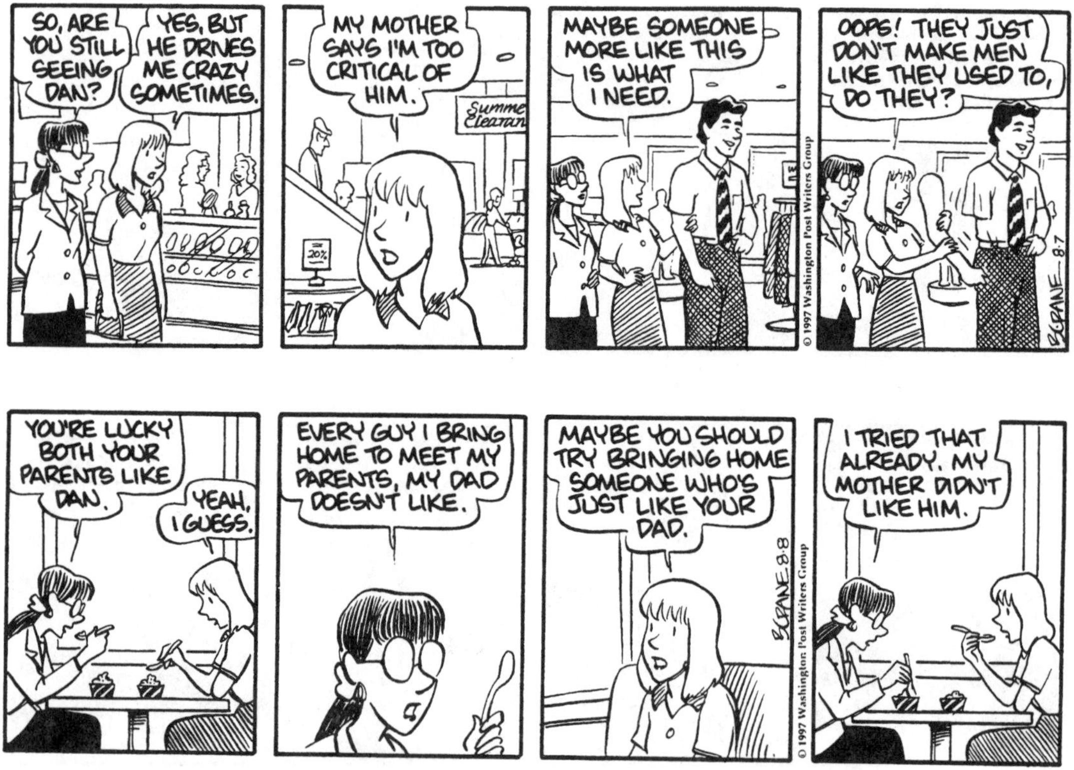
SO, ARE YOU STILL SEEING DAN?
YES, BUT HE DRIVES ME CRAZY SOMETIMES.
MY MOTHER SAYS I'M TOO CRITICAL OF HIM.
MAYBE SOMEONE MORE LIKE THIS IS WHAT I NEED.
OOPS! THEY JUST DON'T MAKE MEN LIKE THEY USED TO, DO THEY?
© 1997 Washington Post Writers Group
YOU'RE LUCKY BOTH YOUR PARENTS LIKE DAN.
YEAH, I GUESS.
EVERY GUY I BRING HOME TO MEET MY PARENTS, MY DAD DOESN'T LIKE.
MAYBE YOU SHOULD TRY BRINGING HOME SOMEONE WHO'S JUST LIKE YOUR DAD.
I TRIED THAT ALREADY. MY MOTHER DIDN'T LIKE HIM.
© 1997 Washington Post Writers Group

PICKLES

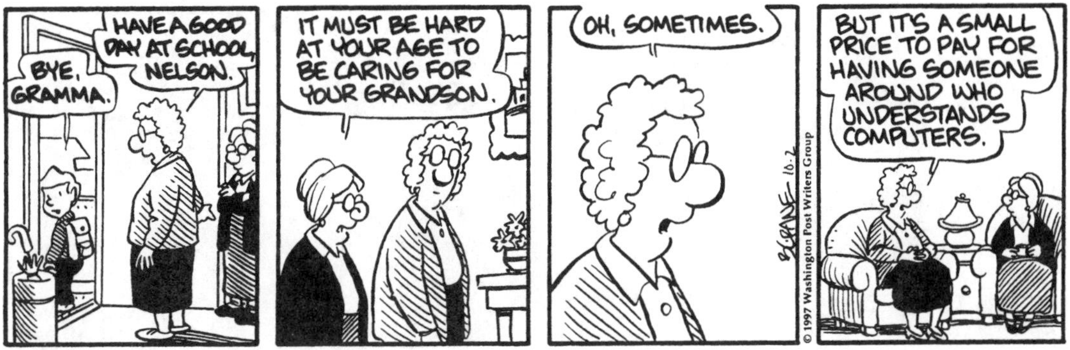

BYE, GRAMMA.
HAVE A GOOD DAY AT SCHOOL, NELSON.
IT MUST BE HARD AT YOUR AGE TO BE CARING FOR YOUR GRANDSON.
OH, SOMETIMES.
BUT IT'S A SMALL PRICE TO PAY FOR HAVING SOMEONE AROUND WHO UNDERSTANDS COMPUTERS.
© 1997 Washington Post Writers Group

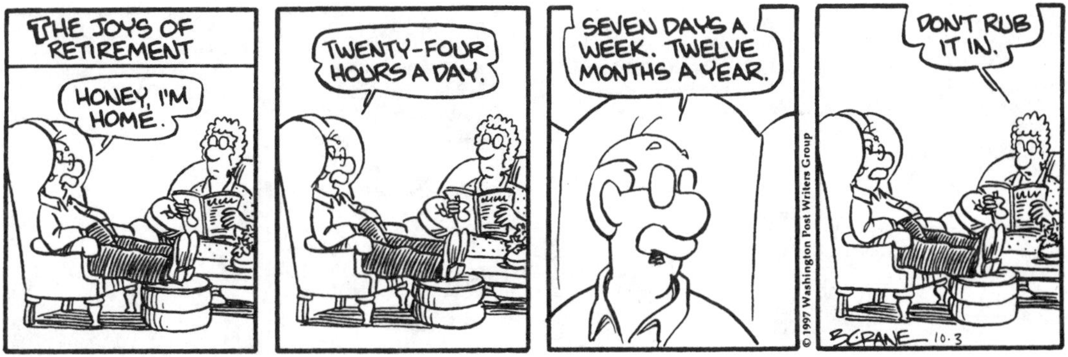

THE JOYS OF RETIREMENT
HONEY, I'M HOME.
TWENTY-FOUR HOURS A DAY.
SEVEN DAYS A WEEK. TWELVE MONTHS A YEAR.
DON'T RUB IT IN.
© 1997 Washington Post Writers Group

PICKLES

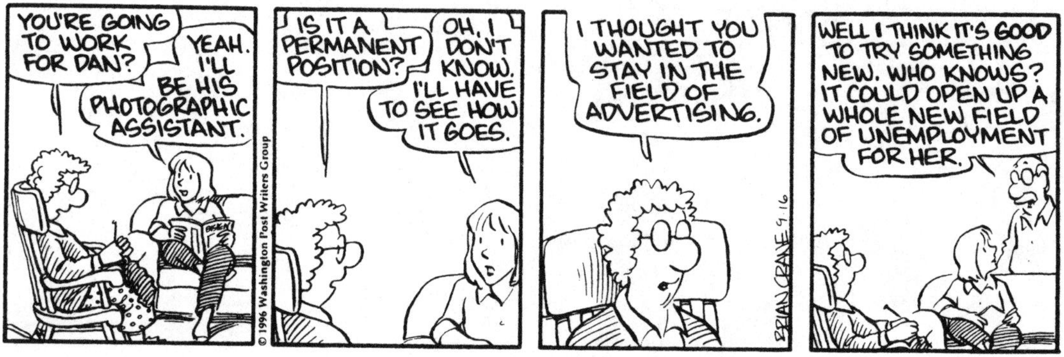

YOU'RE GOING TO WORK FOR DAN?
YEAH. I'LL BE HIS PHOTOGRAPHIC ASSISTANT.
© 1996 Washington Post Writers Group
IS IT A PERMANENT POSITION?
OH, I DON'T KNOW. I'LL HAVE TO SEE HOW IT GOES.
I THOUGHT YOU WANTED TO STAY IN THE FIELD OF ADVERTISING.
BRIAN CRANE 9.16
WELL I THINK IT'S GOOD TO TRY SOMETHING NEW. WHO KNOWS? IT COULD OPEN UP A WHOLE NEW FIELD OF UNEMPLOYMENT FOR HER.

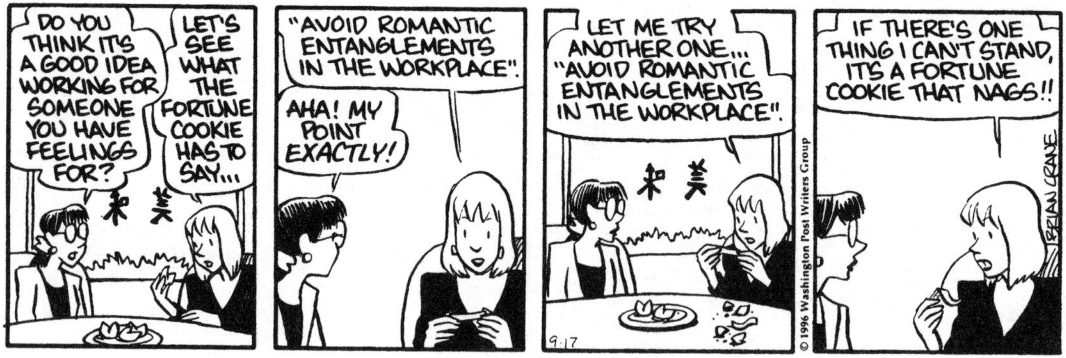

DO YOU THINK IT'S A GOOD IDEA WORKING FOR SOMEONE YOU HAVE FEELINGS FOR?
LET'S SEE WHAT THE FORTUNE COOKIE HAS TO SAY...
"AVOID ROMANTIC ENTANGLEMENTS IN THE WORKPLACE".
AHA! MY POINT EXACTLY!
LET ME TRY ANOTHER ONE... "AVOID ROMANTIC ENTANGLEMENTS IN THE WORKPLACE".
9.17
© 1996 Washington Post Writers Group
IF THERE'S ONE THING I CAN'T STAND, IT'S A FORTUNE COOKIE THAT NAGS!!
BRIAN CRANE

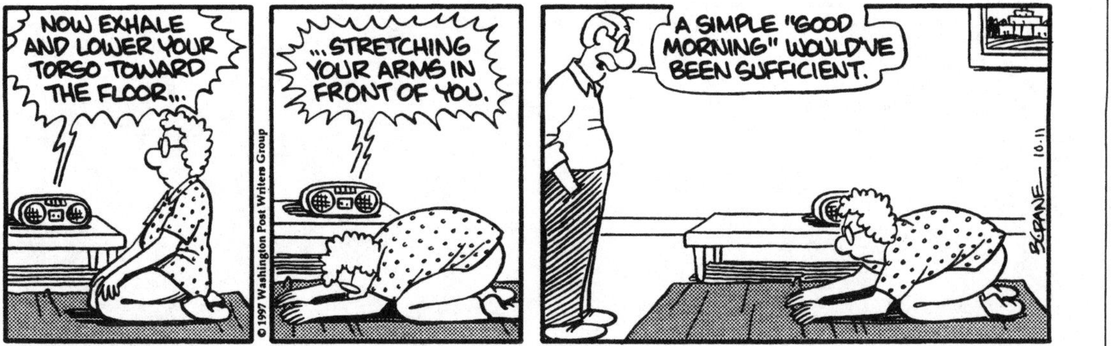
NOW EXHALE AND LOWER YOUR TORSO TOWARD THE FLOOR...
...STRETCHING YOUR ARMS IN FRONT OF YOU.
A SIMPLE "GOOD MORNING" WOULD'VE BEEN SUFFICIENT.
© 1997 Washington Post Writers Group
B. CRANE 10.11

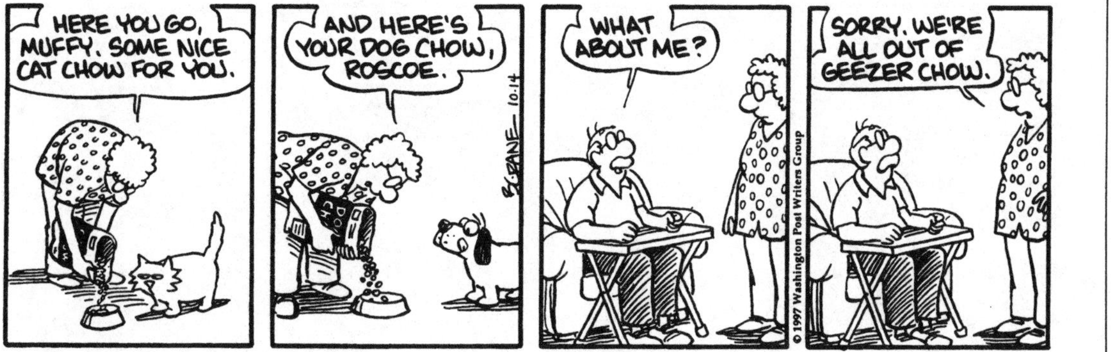
HERE YOU GO, MUFFY. SOME NICE CAT CHOW FOR YOU.
AND HERE'S YOUR DOG CHOW, ROSCOE.
WHAT ABOUT ME?
SORRY. WE'RE ALL OUT OF GEEZER CHOW.
B. CRANE 10.14
© 1997 Washington Post Writers Group

PICKLES

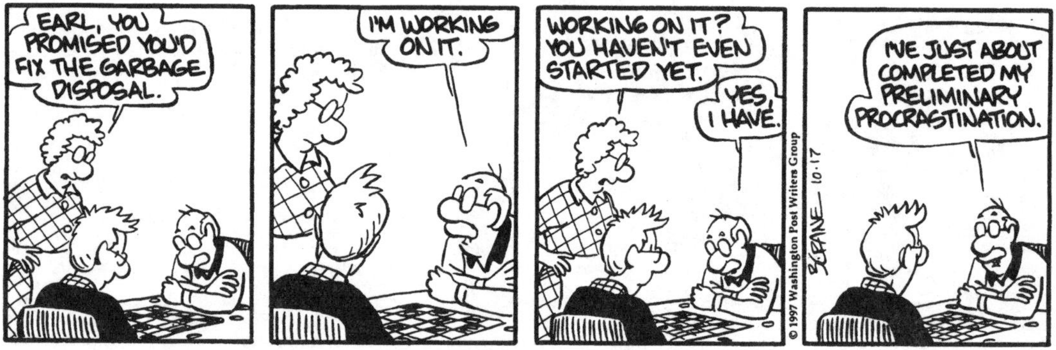
EARL, YOU PROMISED YOU'D FIX THE GARBAGE DISPOSAL.
I'M WORKING ON IT.
WORKING ON IT? YOU HAVEN'T EVEN STARTED YET.
YES, I HAVE.
I'VE JUST ABOUT COMPLETED MY PRELIMINARY PROCRASTINATION.
© 1997 Washington Post Writers Group
B. CRANE 10·17

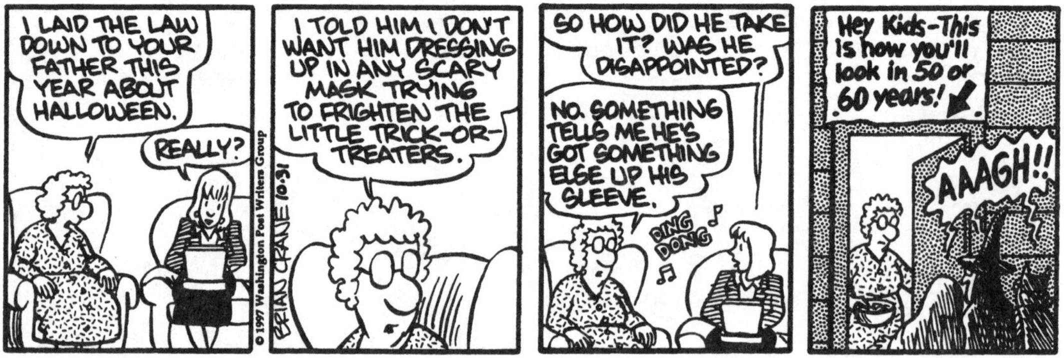
I LAID THE LAW DOWN TO YOUR FATHER THIS YEAR ABOUT HALLOWEEN.
REALLY?
© 1997 Washington Post Writers Group
BRIAN CRANE 10·31
I TOLD HIM I DON'T WANT HIM DRESSING UP IN ANY SCARY MASK TRYING TO FRIGHTEN THE LITTLE TRICK-OR-TREATERS.
SO HOW DID HE TAKE IT? WAS HE DISAPPOINTED?
NO. SOMETHING TELLS ME HE'S GOT SOMETHING ELSE UP HIS SLEEVE.
DING DONG
Hey Kids–This is how you'll look in 50 or 60 years!
AAAGH!!

PICKLES

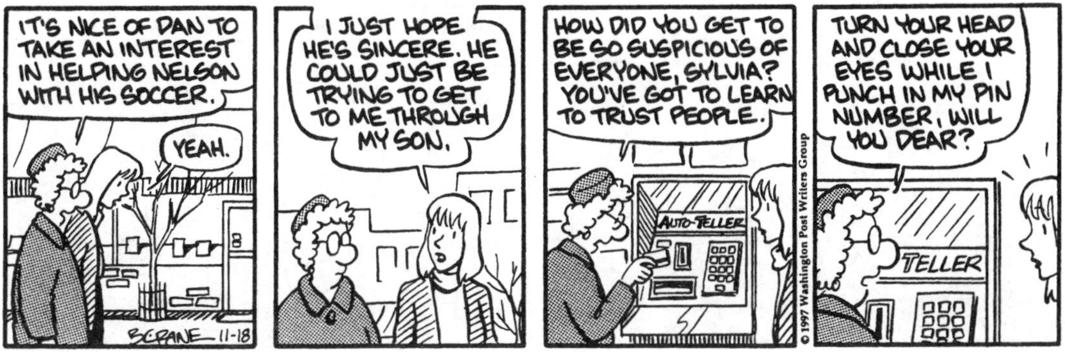
IT'S NICE OF DAN TO TAKE AN INTEREST IN HELPING NELSON WITH HIS SOCCER.
YEAH.
B. CRANE 11-18
I JUST HOPE HE'S SINCERE. HE COULD JUST BE TRYING TO GET TO ME THROUGH MY SON.
HOW DID YOU GET TO BE SO SUSPICIOUS OF EVERYONE, SYLVIA? YOU'VE GOT TO LEARN TO TRUST PEOPLE.
AUTO-TELLER
© 1997 Washington Post Writers Group
TURN YOUR HEAD AND CLOSE YOUR EYES WHILE I PUNCH IN MY PIN NUMBER, WILL YOU DEAR?
TELLER

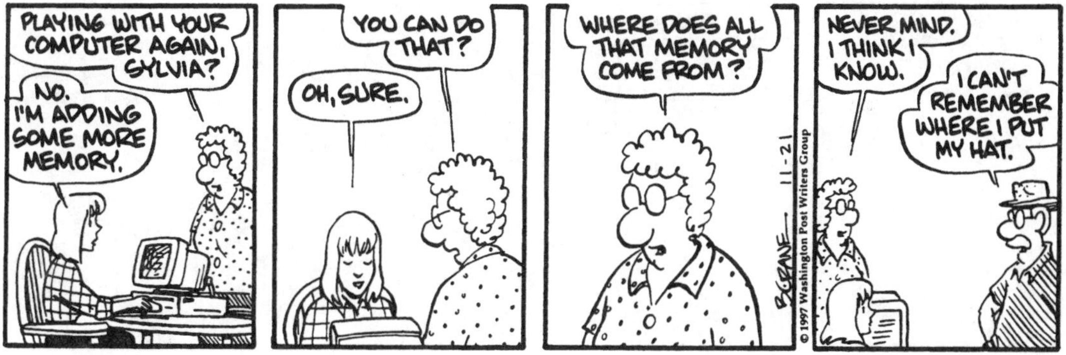
PLAYING WITH YOUR COMPUTER AGAIN, SYLVIA?
NO. I'M ADDING SOME MORE MEMORY.
YOU CAN DO THAT?
OH, SURE.
WHERE DOES ALL THAT MEMORY COME FROM?
11-21
B. CRANE
© 1997 Washington Post Writers Group
NEVER MIND. I THINK I KNOW.
I CAN'T REMEMBER WHERE I PUT MY HAT.

PICKLES

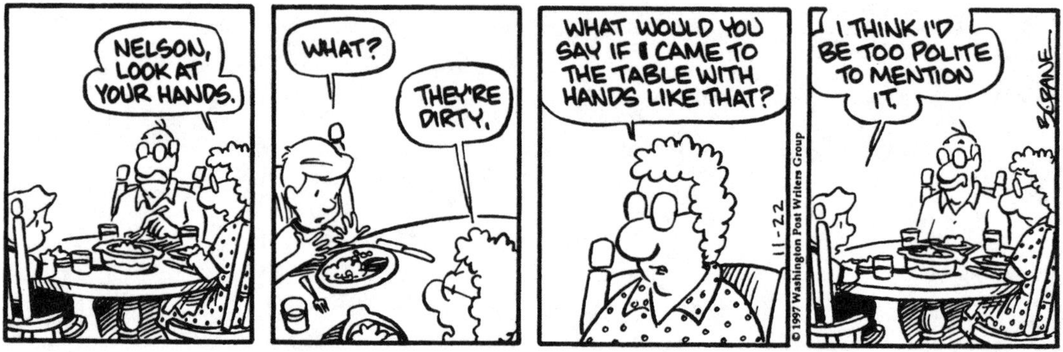
NELSON, LOOK AT YOUR HANDS.
WHAT?
THEY'RE DIRTY.
WHAT WOULD YOU SAY IF I CAME TO THE TABLE WITH HANDS LIKE THAT?
I THINK I'D BE TOO POLITE TO MENTION IT.
11-22
© 1997 Washington Post Writers Group
B. CRANE

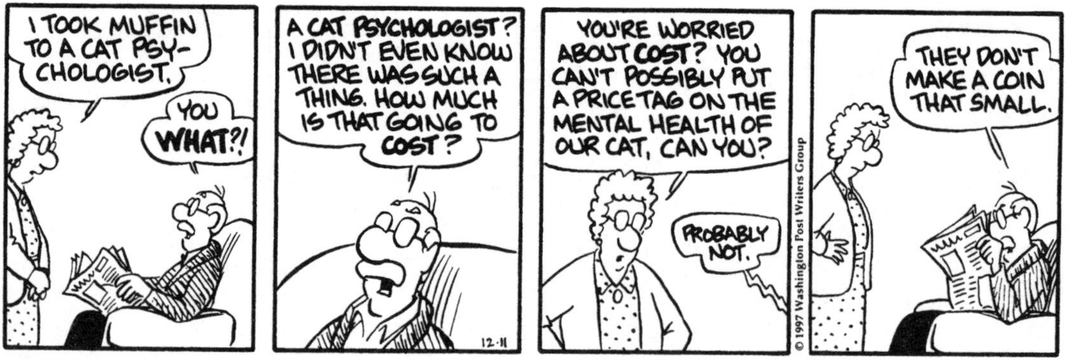
I TOOK MUFFIN TO A CAT PSY-CHOLOGIST.
YOU WHAT?!
A CAT PSYCHOLOGIST? I DIDN'T EVEN KNOW THERE WAS SUCH A THING. HOW MUCH IS THAT GOING TO COST?
12-11
YOU'RE WORRIED ABOUT COST? YOU CAN'T POSSIBLY PUT A PRICE TAG ON THE MENTAL HEALTH OF OUR CAT, CAN YOU?
PROBABLY NOT.
© 1997 Washington Post Writers Group
THEY DON'T MAKE A COIN THAT SMALL.

PICKLES

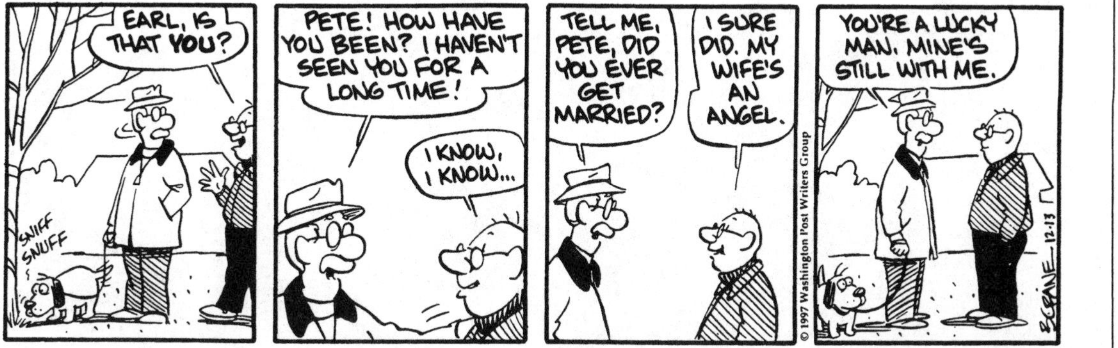
EARL, IS THAT YOU?
SNIFF SNUFF
PETE! HOW HAVE YOU BEEN? I HAVEN'T SEEN YOU FOR A LONG TIME!
I KNOW, I KNOW...
TELL ME, PETE, DID YOU EVER GET MARRIED?
I SURE DID. MY WIFE'S AN ANGEL.
© 1997 Washington Post Writers Group
YOU'RE A LUCKY MAN. MINE'S STILL WITH ME.
12·13
B. CRANE

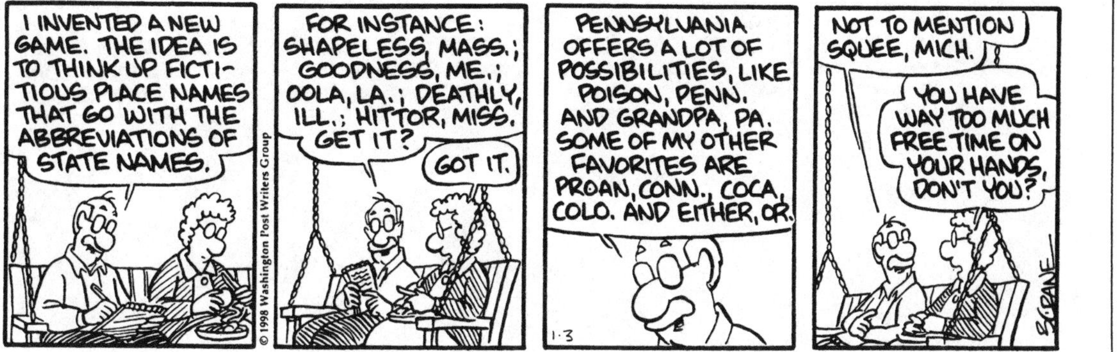
I INVENTED A NEW GAME. THE IDEA IS TO THINK UP FICTITIOUS PLACE NAMES THAT GO WITH THE ABBREVIATIONS OF STATE NAMES.
© 1998 Washington Post Writers Group
FOR INSTANCE: SHAPELESS, MASS.; GOODNESS, ME.; OOLA, LA.; DEATHLY, ILL.; HITTOR, MISS. GET IT?
GOT IT.
PENNSYLVANIA OFFERS A LOT OF POSSIBILITIES, LIKE POISON, PENN. AND GRANDPA, PA. SOME OF MY OTHER FAVORITES ARE PROAN, CONN., COCA, COLO. AND EITHER, OR.
1·3
NOT TO MENTION SQUEE, MICH.
YOU HAVE WAY TOO MUCH FREE TIME ON YOUR HANDS, DON'T YOU?
B. CRANE

PICKLES

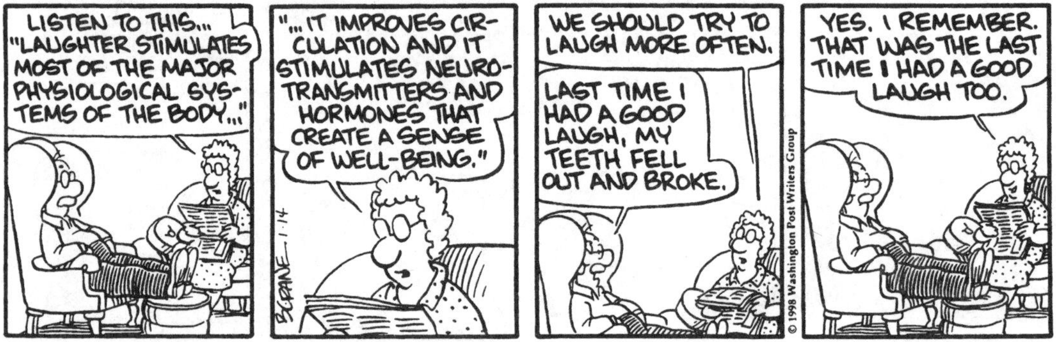
LISTEN TO THIS... "LAUGHTER STIMULATES MOST OF THE MAJOR PHYSIOLOGICAL SYSTEMS OF THE BODY..."
"... IT IMPROVES CIRCULATION AND IT STIMULATES NEUROTRANSMITTERS AND HORMONES THAT CREATE A SENSE OF WELL-BEING."
WE SHOULD TRY TO LAUGH MORE OFTEN.
LAST TIME I HAD A GOOD LAUGH, MY TEETH FELL OUT AND BROKE.
YES. I REMEMBER. THAT WAS THE LAST TIME I HAD A GOOD LAUGH TOO.
© 1998 Washington Post Writers Group

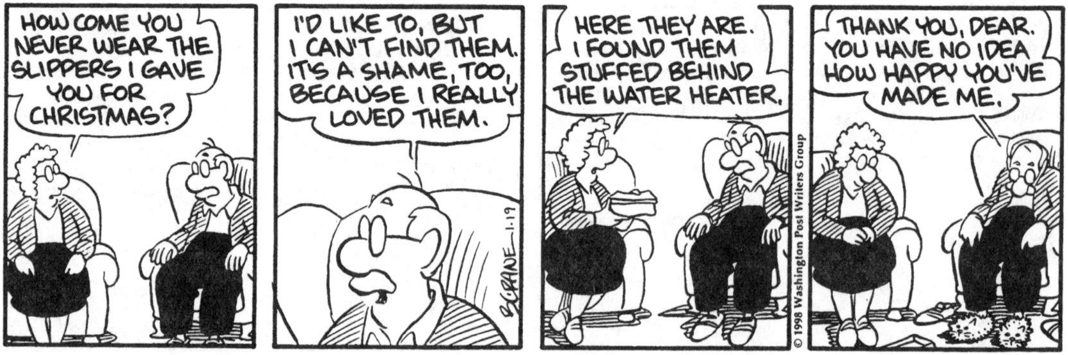
HOW COME YOU NEVER WEAR THE SLIPPERS I GAVE YOU FOR CHRISTMAS?
I'D LIKE TO, BUT I CAN'T FIND THEM. IT'S A SHAME, TOO, BECAUSE I REALLY LOVED THEM.
HERE THEY ARE. I FOUND THEM STUFFED BEHIND THE WATER HEATER.
THANK YOU, DEAR. YOU HAVE NO IDEA HOW HAPPY YOU'VE MADE ME.
© 1998 Washington Post Writers Group

PICKLES

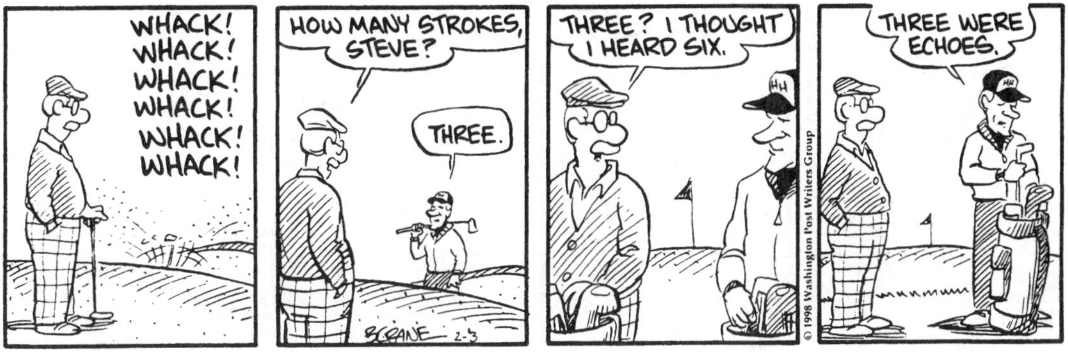
WHACK! WHACK! WHACK! WHACK! WHACK! WHACK!
HOW MANY STROKES, STEVE?
THREE.
THREE? I THOUGHT I HEARD SIX.
THREE WERE ECHOES.
© 1998 Washington Post Writers Group

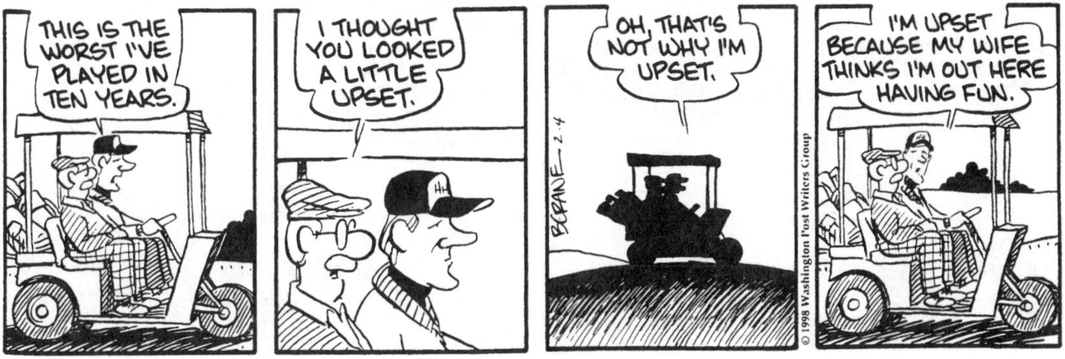
THIS IS THE WORST I'VE PLAYED IN TEN YEARS.
I THOUGHT YOU LOOKED A LITTLE UPSET.
OH, THAT'S NOT WHY I'M UPSET.
I'M UPSET BECAUSE MY WIFE THINKS I'M OUT HERE HAVING FUN.
© 1998 Washington Post Writers Group

PICKLES

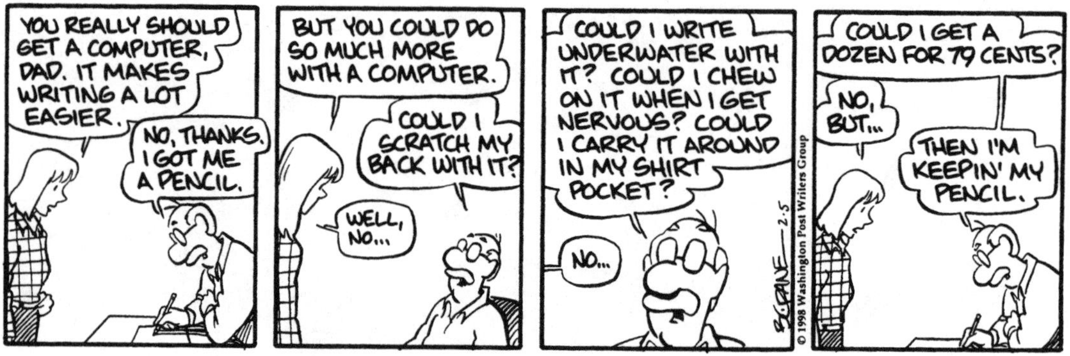
YOU REALLY SHOULD GET A COMPUTER, DAD. IT MAKES WRITING A LOT EASIER.
NO, THANKS. I GOT ME A PENCIL.
BUT YOU COULD DO SO MUCH MORE WITH A COMPUTER.
COULD I SCRATCH MY BACK WITH IT?
WELL, NO...
COULD I WRITE UNDERWATER WITH IT? COULD I CHEW ON IT WHEN I GET NERVOUS? COULD I CARRY IT AROUND IN MY SHIRT POCKET?
NO...
B. CRANE 2-5
© 1998 Washington Post Writers Group
COULD I GET A DOZEN FOR 79 CENTS?
NO, BUT...
THEN I'M KEEPIN' MY PENCIL.

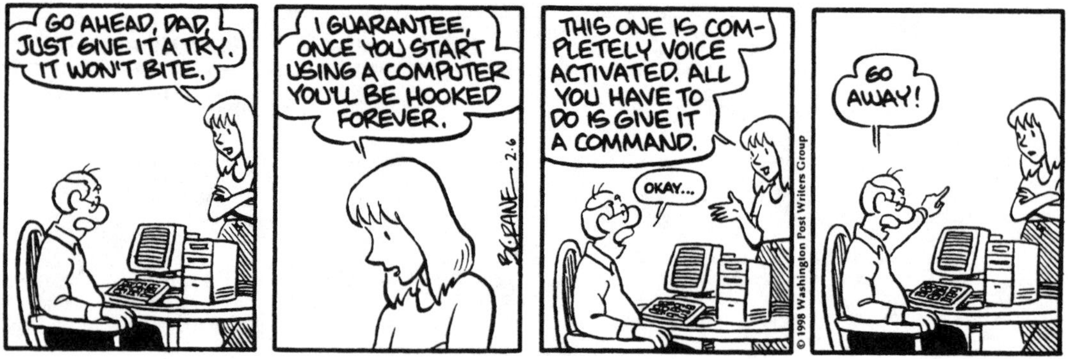
GO AHEAD, DAD, JUST GIVE IT A TRY. IT WON'T BITE.
I GUARANTEE, ONCE YOU START USING A COMPUTER YOU'LL BE HOOKED FOREVER.
B. CRANE 2-6
THIS ONE IS COMPLETELY VOICE ACTIVATED. ALL YOU HAVE TO DO IS GIVE IT A COMMAND.
OKAY...
© 1998 Washington Post Writers Group
GO AWAY!

PICKLES

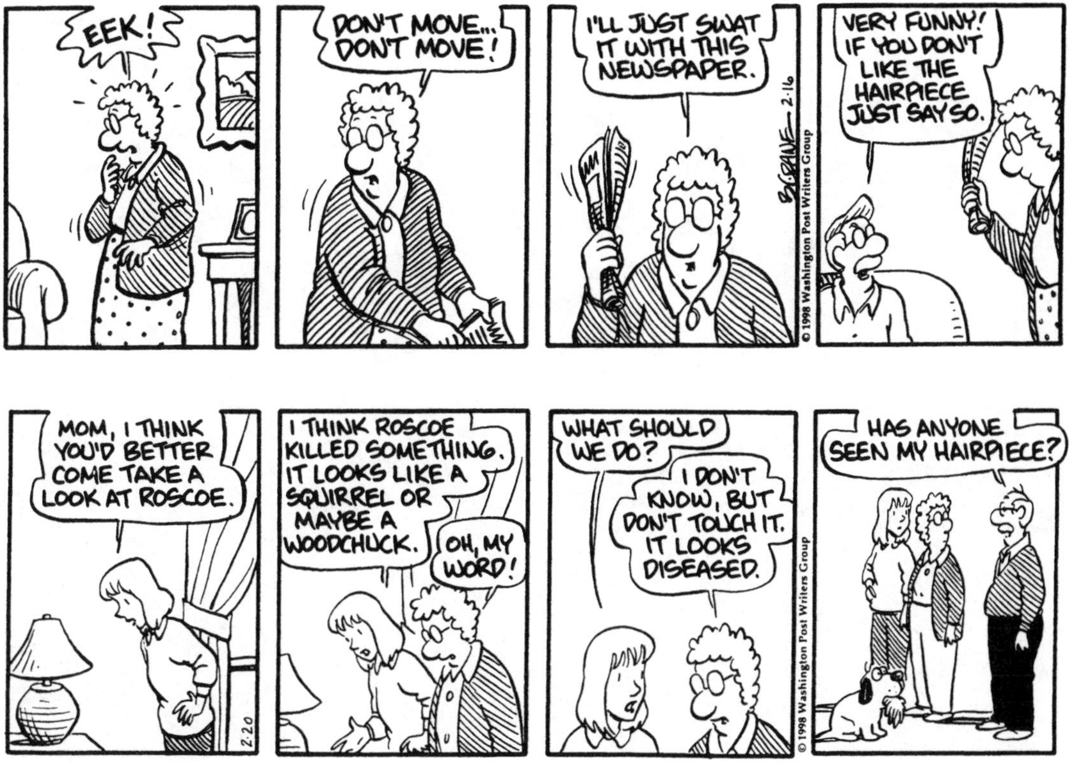
EEK!
DON'T MOVE... DON'T MOVE!
I'LL JUST SWAT IT WITH THIS NEWSPAPER.
2·16
B. CRANE
© 1998 Washington Post Writers Group
VERY FUNNY! IF YOU DON'T LIKE THE HAIRPIECE JUST SAY SO.
MOM, I THINK YOU'D BETTER COME TAKE A LOOK AT ROSCOE.
2·20
I THINK ROSCOE KILLED SOMETHING. IT LOOKS LIKE A SQUIRREL OR MAYBE A WOODCHUCK.
OH, MY WORD!
WHAT SHOULD WE DO?
I DON'T KNOW, BUT DON'T TOUCH IT. IT LOOKS DISEASED.
© 1998 Washington Post Writers Group
HAS ANYONE SEEN MY HAIRPIECE?

PICKLES

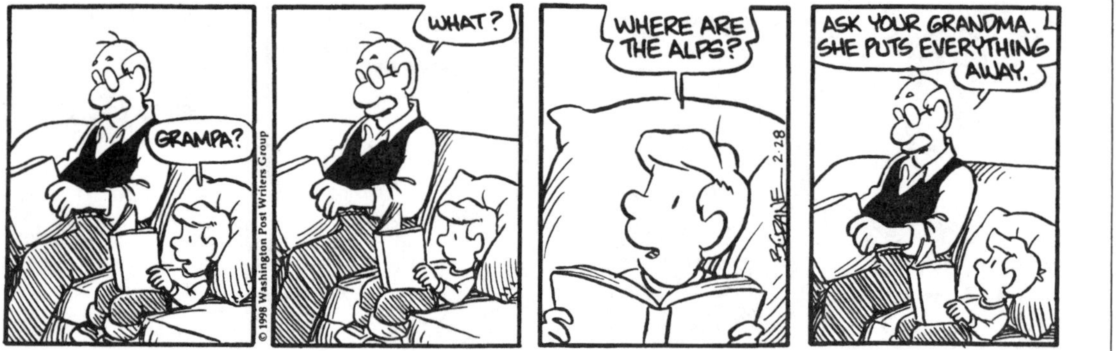

GRAMPA?
© 1998 Washington Post Writers Group
WHAT?
WHERE ARE THE ALPS?
ASK YOUR GRANDMA. SHE PUTS EVERYTHING AWAY.

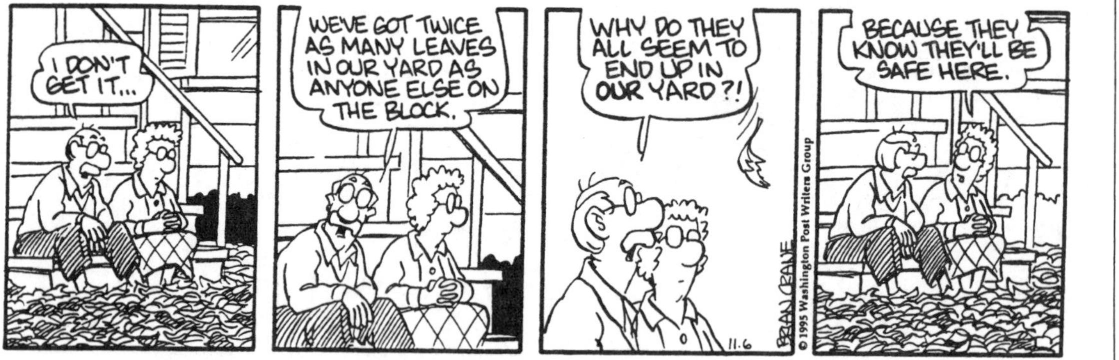

I DON'T GET IT...
WE'VE GOT TWICE AS MANY LEAVES IN OUR YARD AS ANYONE ELSE ON THE BLOCK.
WHY DO THEY ALL SEEM TO END UP IN OUR YARD?!
© 1995 Washington Post Writers Group
BECAUSE THEY KNOW THEY'LL BE SAFE HERE.